I WANT

TO GO HOME

Reclaiming Power After Sexual Assault

Renee Marie Simpson

I have tried to recreate events and conversations from my memories of them. To maintain anonymity in some instances, I have changed individuals' names and identified details to protect their privacy.

This book is not intended as a substitute for the medical advice of physicians. The reader should regularly consult a physician in matters relating to his/her health and particularly with respect to any symptoms that may require diagnosis or medical attention.

Trigger Warning – This book's content will discuss multiple forms of trauma, including intergenerational trauma, sexual assault, rape, self-harm, anti-muslim bigotry, sexuality, racism, lack of food, and mental health. At times, this might be challenging and cause discomfort. It is the reader's responsibility to take care of their experience relating to mental well-being and seek professional support if needed.

Visit the author's website at reneemariesimpson.com

ISBN: 9870646832630

Cover design: Onur Burc

Contents

Introduction

If you've picked up this book, you must've survived. Welcome. You've found a safe place to drop that heavy bag you've been carrying on your back. I wrote this book for you, and I'm glad you went seeking and found it.

I want to take you on a journey to learn how to reclaim power after sexual assault as I share with you how I stumbled across it for myself. I intend to help you find whatever it is you need to take back control over your life. It's time to live again. Life is a gift that must be opened and played with, not tomorrow but *now*. Not to be shelved, unappreciated, and taken for granted, as we do with everything else that matters.

And let's get one thing straight. What happened to us does not define us. It is one part of our story. There is so much more to come, and the best comes after you decide you've had enough of settling and you're ready to put yourself first. Life is short, and we need to get amongst it. Because just like that, lights out. It can be all over in the flick of a switch.

Let's stop wasting time and start getting to work, liberating ourselves from all the bullshit that holds us back, keeps us small, and confines us to victim status. We're better than that. We deserve better than that. And we're going to make damn well sure that we get it, that we earn it without the pity parties. We need to find the power to give it to ourselves—no time for regrets. You have suffered so much already.

Today, I want you to make new choices to prioritise *your*

needs. To live lighter. To follow your passions. To chase those adventures. To seek freedom. To find creativity. To be brave and speak up. Whatever you need in pursuit of your healing, I hope this book helps you find it. I want you to reach a place where you can courageously reflect on your story and discover that life has been beautiful. All of it. Not just the good bits. And not excluding the shit bits.

In the book *Women Who Run With the Wolves*, Jungian analyst, poet, and author Clarissa Pinkola Estes shares "La Loba's Story." It's about a woman who lives in a cave in the mountains and who comes out only on a full moon to collect wolf bones. Clarissa explained that these bones represent our stories. The woman assembles the bones in a skeleton form, and as she does this, she thinks about what song she will sing over them. To me, this represents the song in your heart that we need reminding of when we forget the words. When we lose sight of who we are and what we want from our relationship with life.

The woman sings the song over the bones, which breathes life into the wolf, reviving it. The wolf awakens and runs free into the moonlight. The wolf transforms into a beautiful, naked woman who begins to laugh because she is free.

I believe every one of us can relate to this story in one way or another. Are you the older woman who lives in the cave? Are you the healer? Do you need healing? Do you know your song? Do you know how to sing it? Who can remind you of the words when you forget? Do you know what you need to do to breathe again? Do you remember what it feels like to laugh loudly and run free?

You see, Clarissa Pinkola Estes taught me that our bones are rich with the stories we've collected throughout our lives. But I have discovered that our hearts carry the gentle melodies of the songs that can heal the bones that might feel broken. You no longer need to fear the hard times. Because deep down, you know where to find the trust to breathe life back into yourself—you've done it a million times before, and you will continue to do it a million times again. But sometimes we need some help remembering.

I want you to remember how to revive the parts of yourself which have lain dormant in a culture that fails to support the psychospiritual, vitality, and liberation of humanity. I want to invite you on a journey to reclaim your stolen power. I want you to overcome feeling overwhelmingly helpless, the hopelessness that feels like no one will understand or can help. I want to invite you to explore yourself to learn what medicine you need to save yourself. I want you to flip the script and share stories of good people who've played memorable roles in your healing: the angels who have offered you genuine respect, absolute value, and care.

I want you to tell better stories. Stories about the self-healing power that can happen in our hearts when you learn how to cultivate virtues within. Because none of us are free until we all are, but to free ourselves, we need to speak our truth. Some language in this book might make you feel a little uncomfortable at times, but I've done that intentionally because too often, we pull back from the truth of our stories and the words that push others out of their comfort zones.

I challenge you to sit with any phrases that make you feel uncomfortable—allow them to pierce your skin, flow through your blood, and permeate your bones. Let the monsters come up for air and let them fall away. Facing our truth can be mighty fucking uncomfortable. But we need to learn to get comfortable with the facts.

The stories you will read in this book happened to me, and they have happened to many other people, and they will continue to happen, but that doesn't make them any less essential to talk about and share. We need to learn to sit with the silence in between the songs. It is about learning to speak about what happened. The facts. It is about sharing our stories with people to create a world that doesn't feel so fucking lonely. We need to learn to sit with the uncomfortable to hold space for the truth to support our people.

If we share our stories, I believe we can make a difference in the world. Our stories teach our children how to respect each other. Maybe sharing our stories could plant seeds that make a person think twice about hurting someone. Possibly there will be one less person burdened by the scars that tattoo our souls. We can only try, but it takes bravery to own our stories.

It's time for us to speak up. It is time to demand respect—to have the right to justice, legal ownership of our stories and the right to be heard and believed when we have the bravery to ask for help. It is time for the system that serves to protect us, to do better. And it is time for the wider community to have the courage not to turn away when we speak. We are goddamn motherfucking survivors! And we deserve the space to heal.

We play an essential role within our families, cultures, societies, organisations, institutions, and the systems we belong to. We need to take responsibility as active members of those communities to create safer environmentsfor all. Decision-makers must look at how they can make a deep level change in the attitudes and actions for whom they are responsible. We can not allow sexual assault to remain an invisible issue any longer. We need to act together.

I want to acknowledge and pay respect to all survivors and the stories they hold inside their bones. By sharing our stories, we allow those bones time to bleed, to breathe fresh air into parts of you that might often feel dead. Our stories have the power to teach lessons. Powerful fucking lessons. Lessons that can teach our children to be brave. But first, we have to learn how to speak up. I hope this book helps you find a way to remove the bones that have been stuck in your throat.

I want to honour and pay respect to my younger self as she explored, made discoveries and connections within her worlds. I want to acknowledge the gaps in her awareness, ignorance, and naivety. But just as important, I want to recognise her courage to take risks, to make mistakes, her willingness to learn, and her ability to be honest in how she did it.

I want you to learn how to run by first knowing why you run and where you run to. I've been a runaway in many ways and for so many years, but I also know what it feels like to dance with my demons in the storm and it feels fucking fantastic!

I'm an adventurer. A curious explorer. A seeker of answers. I love to travel and climb mountains around me, but more importantly, I look forward to summiting the many more within. Adventure, to me, is about being brave and taking risks. Owning all of it and then taking responsibility for accomplishing my dreams. And how I love to run. I've just discovered a different direction. I want you to find this too.

Let's go on an adventure together to rediscover what home means for you. I honour the divine spark that is inside of you because it is also inside of me. Namaste.

"Turn your wounds into wisdom."

OPRAH

Step 1. Collect Your Bones

"Loving ourselves through the process of owning our story is the bravest thing we'll ever do."

BRENE BROWN

Chapter 1

It was time to get the fuck out of there. I had grown accustomed to running away when things got too hard. But this time I wasn't running. I was sailing. I needed a place to rest my weary bones. I needed home.

"Aren't you sailing halfway around the world today?" Sean, my friend and housemate, called out from the living room of the houseboat.

My brain felt like it had swollen inside my skull. Why was he yelling at me? I tried to remember how many drinks I had the night before. I needed to start carrying a permanent marker and keep a tally on my arm like my friends, and I did at Oktoberfest in Munich years ago.

In attempting to open my tired, bloodshot eyes, I was blinded by the light reflecting off a neighbouring yacht. I couldn't remember anything—another blackout. I reached for my sunglasses beside the bed and made a mad dash to the fridge, searching for orange juice. I gulped big swallows of the rich pulp, the cold sensation immediately soothing my dry mouth.

"Yes, today is the day! What have I got myself into, mate?" I asked, half-joking, and still half-drunk.

"You'll be right, Nae. The dry boat will be good for you because you wreak of alcohol," he teased, one hand leaning on the door frame of the kitchen.

I laughed, gave him the finger, and headed for the shower. I shrugged off Sean's subtle inference it would do me good being on a boat that didn't allow any drinking by breaking out in song with a mouthful of toothpaste.

"They tried to make me go to rehab. I said, no, no, no!" Amy Winehouse was taken far too young.

I had to admit Sean was right. It was a good time for me to leave. I made excuses to feel okay about why my drinking was increasing. *You're twenty- two and everyone is out of control at this age. It must be because you're bored. You're not enjoying your nights out anymore. You must be tired of living in Gibraltar. You need a new adventure. You need a boyfriend. You miss your friends and family. You'll be fine. You just miss home.* That must be it. Right?

Today I was leaving on a fifty-three-foot Swan sailing boat named *Who Dares Wins*. There was a television program in Australia with the same name, "Who Dares Wins." The host surprised people at work and dared them to do brave acts like skydiving or swimming with sharks. They had to decide on the spot. Yes or no. And off they would go. Funnily enough, my decision to snap up this adventure was quite similar in process.

Over the past six weeks, I worked in a laundrette, saving money to travel to the La Tomatina festival in Spain. One morning, a man in his mid-thirties, shaved head, compact stature, leathery skin the colour of a dark timber stain walked in and introduced himself as Lee.

"I've noticed you work two jobs in Marina Bay. The Ship-Inn pub and here."

"Are you stalking me?" I smiled.

"No, sorry. That came out wrong. I just thought you must know many people around here. Do you know anyone who might be interested in crewing a fifty-three-foot swan sailing boat to Phuket in Thailand?"

"Do they need experience?" I enquired.

"No, I can train them."

"Are expenses included?"

"Yes, all food supplies, visas, and there might be flights at the end."

"Do you take females, and is it a dry boat?"

"Yes, dry boat and happy to take females."

That was my "Who Dares Wins" moment. I thought hard and fast. I missed Steve desperately. Steve was my boyfriend until he suddenly had to return to New Zealand. We decided it was best to part ways. But not a day went by I didn't think of him.

I told Lee I was interested and might know others too, but I needed time to talk to a few people before I made a decision.

"When do you plan to leave?"

"As soon as I can get everything ready on the boat."

I told him I was going to Valencia for a week for a festival. He said he could wait. I thought about my housemate, Nikki. She and I had bonded over our childhood experiences, changing schools, often feeling like social outcasts, and both having distant relationships with our fathers.

Nikki's parents divorced when she was fourteen. She believed her relationship with her father was why she entered a series of what she described as "crappy" relationships. And so, at twenty-three, she ran away from the UK to live in Gibraltar, searching for something else to make her happy, but like most little girls, Nikki just wanted her father's love and acceptance. I recalled her father was now living in Thailand.

After work, I power walked back to the houseboat, eager to tell Nikki about this opportunity that could help her rebuild a relationship with her father.

I arrived home to the smell of something good cooking. I could see Nikki in the kitchen. I almost fell in the water, rushing onto the boat.

"Nikki! Fuck, you are never going to guess what happened today. Are you keen to see your dad in Chiang Mai?" I panted.

"Yes! What the fuck is going on?" Nikki accepted instantly; her big blue eyes wild with excitement. No questions. She was sold.

I told her about my conversation with Lee and pointed out my safety concerns. We made a plan first to get to know Lee and any other crew member. If they checked out, we would speak to Nathaniel and Brad, who owned the local sailing school and ask their opinion.

Nikki and I found Lee's boat easily as it was a small marina, and we knew most of the people who lived there. I introduced Nikki to Lee as a potential crew member, and he invited us onto his boat. Andrew, who much preferred to be called Andy, introduced himself and offered both of us a beer. Andy also sported a shaved head, mid-thirties, tall with a stocky build, with a striking resemblance to professional hockey players you see in the movies.

Lee and Andy were Canadian and had grown up together, but they hadn't seen each other in over fifteen years. Andy had split with his girlfriend, who had just given birth to his first child he lovingly referred to as his "peanut." He needed to clear his head, so he accepted Lee's offer to deliver the boat to Thailand.

Lee had lived in Phuket for some years, working as a skipper on a charter boat for a hotel company. The owners instructed him to fly to Gibraltar and deliver *Who Dares Wins* to expand the hotel's charter business. Lee explained more about his vision for the journey. He estimated it would take two months and told us about the opportunities to stop and explore exotic destinations and cultures, learn to sail, surf, snorkel reefs, and laze around on beaches drinking cocktails. He wrapped it up by mentioning it would also be a lot of hard work. It was a great pitch!

Walking back to the houseboat, Nikki and I agreed that Lee and Andy seemed genuine.

Later that night, we tracked down Nathaniel and Brad at a local bar. Nathaniel and Brad were notorious for trying to pick up young women. A few weeks prior, they invited me and my friend, Lucy, on a day trip to sail to Morocco. It had been my only sailing experience by that point.

They were respectful, but we knew they were just interested in having the company of beautiful young women. They appeared the same age as my step-father back in Australia. I felt like these guys were the closest thing I had to a father figure in Gibraltar. I trusted they might offer some level of care, guidance, and protection, something like my step-father, provided back at home.

I asked them if they could meet Lee and Andy and assess the safety of the boat and the crew. They agreed.

The following night, the six of us went out for dinner and then inspected the boat. I asked our friends for their report.

"If you wouldn't let your own daughter get on the boat, I'm not going!" I declared.

They gave us the green light and reassured us it was an opportunity of a lifetime. In our hearts, we knew this was true, but we needed to think with our heads too. It was one thing to take on an adventure mindset, but it was another thing to rush into situations without proper considerations.

Lucy and I caught up later that night, and I told her about my decision to sail on *Who Dares Wins*. Lucy was excited for me. She had been seeing a guy named Brian, who was in his early twenties and from Germany. I had never really liked Brian much. Lucy had suspected him of cheating on her. He treated me with respect, but I still didn't trust him. His eyes reminded me of snake eyes I had seen at the Australian Reptile Park.

Lucy told Brian about the delivery. He was a fully qualified skipper with plenty of experience. The next day he came into the laundrette and told me he was coming too. Lucy was heartbroken. I felt sad for her, and I knew I had to be nice to Brian now that we were going to sea together.

The morning we left, I called Steve and immediately began to cry. Steve and I had met in the Greek Islands and fell in love. He was living in New Zealand, and by this point, we had been apart for twelve months. I had decided this trip meant a chance for us to be together. I shared my insecurities: I had no idea how to sail or what to expect at sea.

Steve was an adventurous type. He had run marathons, hiked volcanoes in the ice, and had many other wild, daring experiences. Meeting me was probably one of them. He lived to explore. Although he had never sailed before, he told me how jealous he felt about the opportunity that life had presented for me. He tried his best to reassure me I was in safe hands and should embrace the unknown and the adventure as it unfolds.

"Feel the fear and do it anyway." Thanks, Susan Jeffers.

I insisted he tell me if he, too, wanted to make a go of a relationship when I return home. I couldn't go to sea for two months and have these thoughts of not knowing whether he felt as committed as I did about this decision. He told me he would do everything it took to make the relationship work. I felt ten times better after that conversation.

Then I called my step-dad for further reassurance. Dad never lets me down.

"You can get off the boat if you don't enjoy it. Don't worry about money. I've got your back. I'm proud of you, Renee. I will not lie, I miss you, and I'm glad you're coming home. There's nothing to be afraid of. You can handle anything. I know you."

It was everything I wanted to hear. No matter how anxious I am, Dad knows how to soothe me. He knew the song in my heart and how to sing it back whenever I had forgotten the words. At 120 kilos and standing six-foot-three with a heart of gold, friends said Dad looked like the actor, John Goodman.

~

I had one hundred pounds in my wallet and a credit card with a $2,000 limit when I stepped onto the boat that day.

We departed from the marina port just as the sun began to set. I waved goodbye to my friends who came to say farewell. I'm sure they thought that was the last time they were ever going to see me alive. Good vibe music was playing out of the speakers on deck, and no one said a word as we sailed away from the rock of Gibraltar. We exchanged naïve, child-like grins, and nervous giggles.

The weather quickly turned after a colossal grey cloud blanketed the sky. The fantasy had ended. Choppy, confused water promptly followed. The wind rushed into my face like a rude awakening, and my hair became a tangled bird's nest. I began to feel fear creep into the place where excitement had just been only a short moment ago.

Lee told us to go below deck and put on warm clothes, drysuits, and harnesses. We followed orders and scrambled down the companionway, the narrow hallways between different parts of the boat.

Lee asked who we would like to team up with for watches. Brian was the only qualified skipper I knew the most, which wasn't much at all. He had been sailing all his life, so I knew I would be safe teaming up with him. I still didn't know Lee. Andy was inexperienced like Nikki and me. It wasn't rocket science that

Brian was the best pick. Let's face it; I was looking out for number one. I might be a little fucked up, but I certainly wasn't silly. I needed to be resourceful. Brian agreed to partner with me.

I was first to helm. The cockpit kept me physically protected from going overboard. I could steer the boat and observe all critical parts of the vessel from there. I could watch everything around me. Helming involved standing for hours at a time whilst the boat repeatedly rocked and jerked from side to side. It was like trying to grip a steering wheel that had no power steering. And if I let go of the wheel, it would spin wildly out of control, sending the whole boat into imbalance and throwing the crew all over the place, more than likely resulting in injury. A little computer screen on a panel to the left resembled a digital clock that displayed the course we were on. In navigation, the course is distinguished by the compass direction of the craft's bow or nose.

During my first helming shift, we had to cross shipping lanes, which are busy routes in the ocean where container ships transport goods between countries. The traffic was consistent. One ship came a little too close to where we could see her stern all lit up and the bow wave. Luckily, she passed us. It's quite terrifying—without these lights, we would have no sense of position or direction in the ocean.

Thinking about this, I realised that maybe my inner lights were failing because I felt like I had lost my sense of direction in life. I didn't know where I was and which way was my true north.

Just then, Brian walked to the bow and tried to fix the sidelights as they were not working. It suddenly dawned on me the amount of responsibility required to crew a boat. What would I do if Brian fell overboard? I don't remember ever having a safety briefing. For safety reasons, the crew that worked on boats are commonly required to complete their "Day skipper" course. I didn't even know where the life jackets were. Would I need to throw him one of those orange floaty things? I didn't even know what the "thing" was called.

The adrenaline began to course through my veins. I felt hot all over and began to sweat profusely. I started to panic. I wasn't prepared for this. But would I ever be?

Brian attached port (left side) and starboard (right side) lights to the boat. It was dark until he turned them on. As he finished and was coming back, I looked up to see a thick black wave circling the bow of the yacht. It had whitewash teeth and was coming straight towards us. I froze. The wave hit hard, and our galley hatch wasn't shut. Because a hatch is a form of access to the deck (like portholes or windows), an open hatch meant that water gushed straight into the kitchen below.

This shit was as real as it gets. I told Brian he would have to take over. I felt like I was going to throw up, faint, chuck a tantrum, and cry all at the same time. I told him I would stay on watch with him, but I couldn't helm in these conditions anymore. I could think of nothing else but the sweet solace that sleep would bring, or at least that's what I thought.

Chapter 2

Sleeping was almost impossible the first week. I was surprised to learn that sailing boats lean to one side. I felt like I was on some kind of horizontal roller coaster ride. There's this thing called a lee cloth that looks like a cotton hammock that attaches to the bunk. It catches you if you roll out of bed, protecting you from falling onto the hardwood floorboards. I slowly adjusted to the lee cloth method of sleep. It reminded me of what it might feel like to be a baby in a mother's womb. I was surrounded by fluid, comfortable, and safe. I slept happily with earplugs.

Going to sleep, I liked to pretend I was somewhere else. But mostly, I imagined I was safe in the warmth of Steve's strong, loving arms, his barrel chest supporting me from behind as I melt into the softness of his light-tan skin. His brown hair tickling my ear, and his breath hot on my neck.

The weather was still gloomy, and the waves pushed the boat about. The weather seemed to reflect what I was feeling inside—a complete and utter emotional mess. I couldn't muster the courage to go on deck to face the reality of this situation. I needed some "me time" to get my thoughts together. I desperately fought my all-too-familiar feelings to run away from this. It's a wonder I didn't just jump overboard and start swimming home.

I needed time to find acceptance of the new reality I had found myself in. And I needed to muster up the courage to stand up to this challenge. My bag of tricks I had always used to cope were no longer available. There was no oil bath to relax after a hard day. There was little chance of alone time. There was no phone reception to call my support networks. There was no access to free telephone helplines or chat services to talk it out. And there was no alcohol. I was in the middle of the Mediterranean Sea, shitting myself.

I knew I was too afraid to help on the deck, so I contributed to the crew by cooking, starting with breakfast. The boys were grateful and appreciative. Nikki helped me in the kitchen. Noticing I hadn't spoken much for twenty-four hours, Nikki was a bit concerned and checked in on me. I was experiencing intense anxiety. I'm usually very social, so this was unusual behaviour for me. Silence usually indicates I am not happy, unwell, or I am being eaten alive by irrational thoughts. I swallowed a seasickness pill and returned to my cloudy mind, remaining silent all day until it was time to return to my favourite place on the boat: my bed.

Eventually, the weather changed to sunny calm waters. I had time to reset. I smiled a genuine, relaxed smile for the first time. My mood shifted. I started to feel like myself again, and the crew were getting to know each other. I felt a sense of cohesion and connection in the air —my heart had always longed for deep human relationships.

We laughed together. Sweet relief. I began to feel comfortable, more adjusted, and safer, surrounded by nothing but the sea. I breathed the salty air deep into my lungs, a refreshing change from tobacco smoke. I closed my eyes and leaned back to experience the moment fully.

We saw giant dolphins, about three metres long and dark grey. They were doing somersaults and playing around us for half an hour before disappearing.

~

I cooked a potato salad for dinner. I boiled and cut potatoes, and fried onions, garlic, and ham with a splash of milk and olive oil. We didn't have a refrigerator, so there were no cold items available, forcing us to rely heavily on canned food. I scrambled eggs and added them to the drained potatoes, mixing them with mayonnaise. Then I cut avocado and tomatoes to put on top.

Wow! Pretty sure it was the best potato salad I had ever eaten. It made me feel better serving the crew. And, on top of that, I didn't have to clean up the kitchen. I've always hated washing up. We had an agreement. One team cook, and the other clean up. I hadn't spent much time cooking since I had been away from home. I hadn't spent much time eating healthy at all since leaving.

On night watch, I helmed for three hours straight with no sitting down. Brian's face sweated profusely as he told me that on luxury yachts, you could comfortably sit in an enclosed cabin and set the course, and the system automatically helms for you. You could read a book or cook as long as you keep checking that you're still on course. There's no real physical labour. This boat had no shelter, so we were exposed to the open elements of nature as we helmed.

Helming, for me, was a battle of the mind and body. It was this intense style of training and discipline. The tension from gripping the helm tightly would create spasms in my arms and shoulders as I tried my hardest to stay on course. I don't surf, but I imagined keeping my balance whilst trying to helm involved similar skills. Every muscle in my body began to ache. But then the aching became the norm. On top of the physical strain, there was intense *fear*.

My insecurities bubbled to the surface. I was afraid I could not handle the weather conditions. I was fearful of the responsibility of a group of people's lives. I feared fucking up and being chastised. I was scared of the unpredictability of the weather. Maybe I was afraid of life! Perhaps the weather was life! *Was I fearful of what life might throw at me? Was I afraid deep down that I didn't have what was needed to navigate the storms, to take the helm during strong winds, when the sky became dark, and it was hard to see what was coming?* Deep down, I realised I was afraid of the fucking hard stuff.

A sail had come undone during a battering. Brian needed to fold it up, which meant he had to keep his footing to walk the ten metres to reach it and back. I helmed, trying to balance the boat and stay on course. I didn't want him to unclip his harness until I was positive the yacht would not cop a smashing. He timed it well and came back to safety. I tried my hardest to follow Brian's instructions. Brian had this superpower for remaining calm. I told myself to be like Brian and focused on my breathing.

Whilst I was helming, a sheet came loose. It looked like a thick rope being whipped around the deck like I've seen stockmen do to herd cattle on farms. I couldn't run for safety, and the boys were focused on other things. I didn't call for help. I just hunched down to protect myself behind the helm and prayed the rope wouldn't find me. I kept doing my job.

Brian noticed the situation and immediately came to the rescue and tightened the sheet securely. Later, Brian told me I did well in that sticky situation, which made me feel good about myself and softened my walls to want to get to know the crew.

The crew exchanged stories about our families, friends, and life experiences. The crew seemed like-minded: chill, calm, and collected. I was picking up on a common theme that ran throughout each of our narratives; we were all avoiding something. Lee was avoiding returning to work. Andrew was avoiding his relationship break up. Brian wanted to avoid settling down in one place. Nikki was avoiding going back to the UK, and

I Want To Go Home

I was avoiding the truth.

~

One week before I flew overseas to Gibraltar, I had gone to a party at the home of my best friend Bree and her boyfriend Ryan. She and I had been close friends since we were thirteen. I adored her, and we told each other everything. I remember her getting pregnant when she lost her virginity at fourteen. She had to have an abortion. She was the first of our friendship group to lose her virginity, and her experience frightened us all to stay clear of sex until we were over sixteen. I loved and respected her for going through such a challenging experience at that age.

When I was seventeen, I used to sneak into our local club through a vacant block. I would swing myself around the fence and walk along a tennis court fence line, being careful not to fall in the water as it was right on a lake. It was quite some effort, and I would have to hold my heels in one hand and hold on to the fence with the other. It was during this time Bree started seeing Ryan. He was a nice guy. Always sweet to Bree and kind to her friends. They moved in together not long after and had been together for about four years.

Bree told me the party was going to be a big night. At twenty-one, everyone was experimenting with ecstasy and drinking alcohol. I passed out in a downstairs room I shared with a big group of friends.

I recall a voice saying, "Hey guys, sleep upstairs."

Half asleep, they walked upstairs without any concern for me, still lying on the floor. I couldn't move. I passed out again.

When I woke up in the morning, my skinny black jeans were on backwards.

What happened?

Something felt very wrong. *Why was I all alone in this room downstairs?* We were a close group of friends who always stayed with each other.

I walked into Bree's room to find all the girls sleeping in there. "Why are my pants on back to front?"

Instead of offering to help solve the mystery of how my pants somehow came off whilst I was sleeping and put back on the wrong way, my "friends" laughed in amusement. No one seemed concerned but me.

I sobered up and drove home.

A memory from the previous night flashed in my mind; A voice said, "It's okay, Renee. It's just me."

And then I remembered his body lying on top of me and not being able to move. He had control of my body. I couldn't cry out for help, and I couldn't say, "Stop."

I couldn't scream, "No, get off me!"

I couldn't speak. I was helpless.

And that's when he raped me, as I was passed out on the floor in the room downstairs.

Did someone spike my drink? I started to blame myself for taking ecstasy and drinking. I questioned whether it was my fault somehow. *Had I been too nice to him? Was it my clothing?* I wore fucking jeans, though! *Did I give him the wrong impression? What did I do wrong to deserve this?*

All I could hear was his voice lingering in my head and breathing on my neck. And I knew that voice.

It was Ryan.

I had my period, and as soon as I got home, I went to the bathroom to check to see if he had taken out the tampon. He didn't.

My best friend's boyfriend raped me with a tampon inside me

by someone I thought was my friend.

I didn't know what to do. I was just about to leave on a trip of a lifetime. Rape response was not part of the plan. I couldn't deal with this right now. I questioned telling someone or going to the police. I wondered about leaving on my trip and pretending it never happened. I thought about keeping it a secret and never tell a soul, or whether I should tell Bree.

I showered and spent the week in my room in shock, crying, and blaming myself. I couldn't look at my family when I came out to get food. They knew something was up but didn't know how to ask me. It took three days for the tampon to come out. Every day I could smell its stench. That smell became the engulfing stench of shame.

A few days before my going away party, I decided I had to do something —the right thing to do was to tell Bree.

I drove to Bree's house, but no one was home. I felt irritated and yet somewhat relieved. I hadn't thought it through. I had no idea what I was going to say or how she might take it.

I had another friend, Michelle, who lived across the road from them. She had been at the party too. I had to tell someone, so I knocked on her door. Michelle answered and invited me in when I burst into tears on her front step. I told her what Ryan had done to me at the party. She wasn't surprised. She said Ryan made her feel uncomfortable too. I asked her what I should do. Michelle advised me to tell no one and to go on with my trip travelling abroad. She said Ryan's group of friends would destroy my reputation. They would make me out to be a liar and blame it on me. She believed the most loving thing I could do for myself was to run away and pretend it never happened.

I'm not sure what I was looking for at the time. *A friend to support and encourage me to go to the police?* It was such an inner conflict because I was friends with these people who knew him. Just twenty-four hours ago, he had been my friend. I couldn't have gone to the police. I wouldn't, and I guess that's why I didn't. I'm not saying this was the right thing to do. I wish I had the strength to go to the police. I have so much respect for people who find the courage to report sexual assault. And I'm sure if someone had asked me the day before this happened what I would have done in this situation, I would have said I would report it to the police, but really, you don't know what you will do until you've experienced it for yourself.

So, I said nothing. I ran away with the secret. A secret that remained lodged in my throat and my nightmares the entire eighteen months I was away from home leading up to the sailing trip. I wish I had respected myself enough to report it. I wish I had understood just how serious the crime was. I wish I had known how detrimental the rape was going to be to my health. How it destroyed the trust, I had in myself, my self-worth, and my sense of safety, particularly in my relationships with men. It became a destructive force that would turn me not against the world or the man who did it but purely against myself. I had been running from it this whole time, and I was getting tired of running.

Step 2. Assemble Your Skeleton

"To be ourselves causes us to be exiled by many others, and yet to comply with what others want causes us to be exiled from ourselves."

CLARISSA PINKOLA ESTES

Chapter 3

Before bed, I rinsed my mouth with salt water after noticing that my gums felt tender but thought nothing of it. Later, in the early hours of the morning, I woke up alarmed by the taste of blood in my mouth. I leapt out of bed to switch on the light. There was blood smeared all over my hands with several bloodstains on my pillow. I ran to the mirror. Blood smudged my face. I opened my mouth and noticed my gums were bleeding profusely.

I didn't know what to do, so I woke Brian for help. I felt nauseous from the sight of the blood. Lee and Brian sought advice from a medical book onboard, while I began to laugh because I looked like a zombie. They informed me it must be gingivitis, an inflammation of the gums caused by a bacterial infection.

How embarrassing. I wasn't a grub. I brushed my teeth twice a day. Fair enough, I had been a little bit neglectful when it came to eating fruit and vegetables. But no one I knew was eating fruit and vegetables. Well, not that I noticed. We didn't have a kitchen in London to cook anything healthy, so I lived off kebabs and samosas. Fruits and vegetables were too expensive. I had to save money. Smoking half a pack of cigarettes a day probably didn't help.

I must have picked up the bacteria at the La Tomatina festival, where you end up wading shin-deep in tomato pulp. It gets dirty fast. It was a festival. But seriously, gingivitis?

If left untreated, it can cause injury to the soft tissue and bone supporting the teeth, as the gums separate from the teeth, and can even cause tooth loss requiring a dental expert to remove. Once again, I washed my mouth with saltwater, massaged my gums, and stayed away from solid food. I changed my pillowcase and went back to bed to try and sleep.

I continually swished salt water in my mouth. It hurt to smile, talk, and eat. It got progressively worse by the day.

Another not-so-welcome messenger popped up: a cold sore right under my nose. I felt like a walking disease. Talk about a wake-up call. My body was seriously yelling out for help. I had been running away from myself for so long I had made myself sick. I had been numbing myself with alcohol from actually feeling anything meaningful. Pretending to drown out the pain by dancing on bar counters and taking off my clothes with other sweaty twenty-somethings. I had made travel into a false paradise, but in fact, it was a cave to keep my secret, and now it was festering from within, oozing out in blood and cold sores carving up my face. I had to start speaking up, telling the truth and owning the reality of my story. I had to start learning how to trust again.

The truth is, the rape wasn't the first time somebody had sexually assaulted me. I was six the first time it happened. I was abused by an elderly neighbour until I was seven. At eight, I told my mum after learning from a movie that what the man did to me was a crime.

I look back on the eight-year-old me. She was strong and demanded my mother take me to the police to report it. I wanted to stop other young girls from experiencing what I had. But it wasn't the sexual assault that left the most significant wound; it was the feeling of being abandoned by the woman I trusted the most: my mother. I suffered because of my mother's childhood trauma. She too had been sexually abused. But her story is not mine to share. What *is* my story, is how it affected *me*.

In every way you can imagine, she was a great mother and my best friend. But when it came to her trauma, her fear crippled her. She didn't want to remember what happened to her. And my experience triggered her in ways she felt she couldn't cope with. And she stopped me from having my day in court, denying my right to justice. This is an example of what the generational trauma cycle looks like, and it's not the survivor's fault, but it passes on the pain to their children. And this is why it was important for me to heal my wounds to provide my unborn children with a safe home and a healthy future.

That experience had an enormous impact on my willingness to trust others for support and protection. Extreme independence was my answer. I decided if I would survive this life, I had to learn to rely solely on myself.

I had been building this trust in myself my entire childhood and adolescence until I was twenty-one, mostly to protect myself from disappointment and hurt. I felt prepared, confident, and wholeheartedly trusting of myself, ready to leave and travel independently overseas. And then the rape happened.

It stole every star in the universe that made up that sky of trust I had worked so hard to create for myself. And now I was in the dark with no stars to guide me home, no light to keep me safe.

It's never the actual physical act of sexual assault that leaves the most prominent scars. It's the emotional and the mental impact that does the damage, and that's what we have to learn to survive.

Now, on the boat fighting gingivitis and cold sores, it made sense why I was experiencing this health crisis. It felt like that wounded eight-year-old child inside me was yanking on my shirt, begging me to put her first, to fight for her, to help heal her. But I had to stop drowning out her cries for help. My ill health was her way of saying, "Renee, I want to go home."

I was beginning to hear her, and I planned to find a way to get there.

The taste in my mouth was revolting, not to mention the foul smell that lingered on everything I seemed to touch. I tried my best to brush my teeth, and I rested in bed. I could hardly talk due to the swelling, so I used sign language and writing to communicate. No solid food. Soup only. Tiny sips of water.

Lee gave orders for me to stay out of the cold because that's when my mouth would bleed the most. Blood congealed between my teeth. The crew helped cover my watches because it was too painful for me to be on deck. The wind sent electric shocks through my gums.

I felt guilty for being so unwell.

The crew suggested I watch a funny movie to take my mind off things, but they didn't know the other demons I was battling inside, the real truth behind why I was sick. And I wasn't ready to speak about it to them. It wasn't about them. It was about me facing it head on.

The engine failed. *That made sense too.* My body showed me I was breaking down, and now the fucking boat was breaking down. I received the message loud and clear. I didn't know if the engine would be easy to fix or not. I knew nothing about motors or boats, so I couldn't do anything to help. But I could try to understand how to start fixing *me*.

Lee and Brian managed to get the motor running again. I felt relieved and took it as a sign I, too, would find a way. Lee asked me if I wanted to go ashore and get medicine at Palma, the capital and largest city of the Balearic Islands in Spain.

With no hesitation, I said, "Yes, please!" I felt like I was dying.

I was thrilled at the idea of getting medicine. I showered on deck, put on the prettiest summer dress I owned, and made myself soup. Lee burst my bubble of hope. We couldn't go to Palma because it would cost too much money to dock.

I was fucking furious. I wished Lee had said nothing to me. I was fragile. The thought of tasting blood for another three or four days made me cry. Tears ran down my dry, dehydrated face—I was uncomfortable being in this vulnerable position.

All hope had abandoned me as I slipped into a state of depression. I wondered what I had done to deserve this. I was envious of the rest of the crew enjoying solid food. I wished I had never stepped a foot on this boat. I started thinking Gibraltar wasn't that bad; at least I could see a doctor there. *Fuck every inspirational person I had ever met, fuck everyone who encouraged me to travel, and fuck all those assholes who told me to go sailing.* I hated everyone.

To take my mind to a happier place, I daydreamed about the time I met Steve on the party island of Ios in the Greek Islands. Steve called out to me from the steps outside a club. After too much to drink, the streets became a labyrinth, and I couldn't find my way back to my accommodation. I was so angry at myself for drinking so much and becoming so disorientated. I told myself that I needed to stick with the group and take better care of myself.

"Hey, you look lost. Where are you staying? Come, I'll help you get back to your accommodation."

Steve was lovely and charming. He held my hand so I wouldn't trip on the cobbled stone path. I told him where I was staying—instant trust.

"Okay, it's too dangerous for you to walk all that way tonight. How about you come back to my hotel, I'll make us a drink, and you can crash there. I have to work in the morning, but I'll draw you a map to get back."

Damn, he was smooth.

It was a beautiful warm night, and the walk back to his hotel sobered me up. Steve was working the season as a bartender. It felt like the whole island had fallen asleep, or more likely passed out, by the serene quiet surrounding me as I sat by the pool waiting for Steve to make me a Pina Colada. We sat on the veranda outside his room. He serenaded me with stories of his adventures, and they were extensive. I told him about mine. I was green in comparison as I had only been away from Australia for one month. I was flat out, floor-to-wall in awe of him.

His eyes locked onto mine, and then he kissed me.

He pulled his mattress out onto the veranda as the sun began to lovingly light up the deep blues and bright whites of the houses that overlooked the Mediterranean Sea. He put his arm around me as a light breeze caressed my skin. His body felt strong yet incredibly soft. I wanted to record his voice and listen to it for hours. He teased that I had an accent. He was kind. Generous. Strong. I had never met anyone I liked so much in just one hour.

I surrendered like a lotus flower at dawn.

Steve's eyes were like oceans of dark hazel that washed away my insecurities. It was just us. Nothing else mattered. We made love as the sun rose beside us, blessing the fusion of our bones with her glow that reflected off our naked bodies.

Steve and I spent every day together for four days, and every night we fell asleep in each other's arms on that balcony.

Replaying that memory eased my pain and gave me hope. I found comfort in realising that if I had allowed the rape to destroy every star in my sky, I never would have left Australia, and I would never have met Steve and shared the most romantic week of my life. There must still be some stars left inside me somewhere.

It was going to take four days until we reached Malta. I just needed to keep my mouth disease under control until then. Then it was only four days until Egypt.

Chapter 4

On land, I felt disconnected from my body. Maybe I turned that connection off. If I could disconnect myself from my body, then perhaps I wouldn't have to remember what happened to it. There were many opportunities to distract me from listening to what my body needed from me. At sea, there were no distractions at all. I had the time, space, and silence to be able to connect with myself as I had never been able to before.

There was no wind in the sails on the eighth night. It felt like we were getting nowhere. I started crying as soon as I woke up. I had been eating pain killers like lollies, but this had to stop.

I needed to speak up and demand help because my health was important. My life was of value. I asked Lee if we could go to the nearest port. I couldn't take the pain anymore. I felt like my body was dying. My mouth was continually burning, and the infection swelled my lips and cheeks. I felt holes in my gums next to my teeth like somebody had poured acid into my mouth overnight. I needed urgent medical attention. The smell was as horrendous as rotting roadkill; I could smell it on everything I touched. Living inside my wretched body had become a curse. I laid on the sofa, praying for God to show herself. I needed her help, gravely.

Lee planned a course to take me to Sardinia by morning. Thank you, God. Lee told me the people in Sardinia speak Italian. I was hanging on by one thread, and I imagined all the people that love me, and I placed them in a circle to help me through the pain. There was Jacqui, Veronica, Todd, Rick, and Rachel. Real friends who came to see me off at the airport when I left Australia. Veronica and Rachel even came to visit in London. I imagined the words of encouragement they might say, and it helped. I longed for the care of my mum and step-dad. I would have paid anything to get help. Whatever it took. I wanted to eat, talk, smile, and even just enjoy the experience. I tried to think about people out in the world who were suffering in worse pain than I was. That helped a bit too.

To cheer me up, Brian encouraged me to write about Steve in my journal. A month after we met, Steve and I met up in London. I was so nervous, doubting he would even still be attracted to me. Fortunately, he was. We fell utterly in love. He showed me how to live on a shoestring budget in London. He showed me where to shop for cheap food, clothes, and alcohol. I learned which buses to catch, and Steve walked me to all of my job interviews, where he waited until they finished. He also helped me choose interview outfits. He always had encouraging words to say. We shoplifted together a few times. I took care of him after a motorbike hit him. He would read me TNT articles about travel as he drank coffee in the mornings. We partied as much as we made love, which was as often as we could, and we never fought, not once. I respected that he made me feel safe. Our love felt indestructible. Steve received news that his father had died, suddenly bringing our time in London together to a close.

Nursing a broken heart, we tried to continue a long-distance relationship, writing letters, sending gifts, staying up late to chat on Messenger, but it wasn't enough for either of us. I wanted to be present in London, but I couldn't yearn to be with him when he was halfway around the world. We agreed it wasn't fair and we should move on.

I gave my journal to Brian to read what I had written. He

smiled and asked if I wanted a hug. It was a sweet offer, considering I knew I was looking, feeling, and smelling like near death. It was lovely to be held, even just for a moment, in arms that reminded me of Steve's. Brian had been taking care of me. He asked questions about how I was feeling, sleeping, and if I needed anything.

Brian woke me and showed me land in the early hours of the morning. I could see a beautiful dark coastline with a few scattered lights that glowed with hope. The sky was getting lighter. The wind was cool against my skin. Pale blue sky peeked behind the dark black silhouette of coastline against the black calm water with tiny ripples. The only white was coming from our wake as we quietly soared through the water. I felt overcome with relief and gratitude. I was eventually going to get help. I tried to avoid getting my hopes up just in case I wasn't able to see a doctor or a dentist to get medicine, but I tried to stay positive.

Who Dares Wins sailed safely into port. Lee told the coast guard we were just stopping for an emergency to prevent being lumped with a docking fee. I was filled with anticipation to get better.

As soon as I stepped off the boat, I felt dizzy and groggy. I had been lying in the same place for twenty-four hours and hadn't eaten for two days. The lack of energy hit me now that I was on land; however, I wasn't relieved to be off the boat either, which struck me.

The coast guards offered to drive us to the hospital. I asked Brian if he would like to come with me. He agreed, offering to hold my hand if I was scared. I glanced at him with appreciation and gently reached out my hand with my palm facing up. He rested his hand upon mine with a gentle squeeze. I squeezed back.

At the hospital, I was rushed straight in. The doctor took one look at my teeth, prescribed a painkiller, antibiotics, and an oral anti-inflammatory. Because of the language barrier, it was difficult communicating with the doctor, but we eventually seemed to understand one another.

The doctor gave me a needle in my bum. I told Brian not to look as I pulled down my pants. He made some inappropriate joke about small pricks, but I was too concerned about the needle the doctor was holding in her hands. I thought she wanted to put it in my gums. Instead, she laid me on my stomach and gently pierced the skin. I started to feel numb, and the medicine carried away my pain.

Luckily, there was one pharmacy open on a Sunday. My angels were looking out for me. We picked up the prescription, and I was sorted and on the road to health. Brian continued to hold my hand on the way back to the boat. He was so supportive. The coast guards drove us back to port. I hopped back on the yacht without hesitation, and we headed off for Malta.

I was determined to get better and enjoy the rest of the trip. The doctor said to expect a week to recover to full health.

Realisation set in that maybe my unhealthy choices had caught up with me. Sickness is what happens when you treat your body like shit. When you abuse drugs, alcohol, smoke, and don't eat well.

Lee let us know it should take about four days to reach Malta. I was looking forward to exploring a new country and culture.

After Sardinia, Brian started to ask me some big questions on watches, challenging my thoughts about Steve.

One night out of the blue, he said, "Do you hear yourself? How you speak about Steve? You've turned him into some god. Does this Steve have any faults? Problems? Is there anything you don't like about him? Do you even know this Steve that well? It sounds like you've built him up in your head, and I'm not sure this guy will meet those expectations. Are your expectations of this relationship and Steve even realistic?" with one hand on the helm and looking out at sea like he was deep in thought.

He didn't take a breath. "Yes, you have had this wonderfully romantic, dreamy experience, but that's what happens when you get swept up at the beginning! What happens when he becomes a human being with flaws and when he fucks up? When he hurts you, when he disappoints you, when he shows you all of himself, not just the good bits? When he becomes a real man to you? What happens then, Renee? Open your eyes. Why do you really want to go home? Be honest with yourself. Because I'm not convinced, it's Steve."

I fell silent. Brian was right. His confronting tone made my eyes water.

"Oh shit, I'm sorry. That was too much," Brian said as he reached out for my hand.

"Can I get back to you on that one? I need to think about what you've just said. But it wasn't wrong. I think your words exactly what I needed to hear. Thanks."

He couldn't take it back, and I couldn't pretend I never heard him say it, nor did I want to. I just had to make sense of it for myself. I had been putting Steve on a pedestal. *What would happen when he became human instead of this figure of worship?*

I realised I was setting myself up for heartbreak. I hadn't seen him for twelve months. *Will I feel differently about him when I see him? What if I am more in love with missing him than the reality of being with him?*

I wasn't sure how to answer Brian, so I didn't. But I was grateful for his perspective.

Chapter 5

Andy helmed for the duration of the sunlight hours when I was sick. He kept a close eye on me when I started to get better.

In a tone only a father could have, he reminded me, "Take it easy, Renee. You just take it easy, okay?"

He told me it scares him to think that his "peanut" could ever be in the same position as I was a few days ago. If only he knew the whole truth.

It wasn't long before I returned to work with the crew. I cooked every meal they would allow me to and did all the clean-up. I gave the crew my carton of cigarettes. If one of them wanted a smoke, I would light it. I helmed for as long as I could every watch. I gave Brian massages. I washed Nikki's clothes. I helped the crew apply sunscreen. I made tea and coffee for everyone every half hour. I cleaned the galley. And I never complained once. I wanted to give the crew my all to show them just how grateful I was for their support.

I was over the moon; the medicine worked fast, and in no time, I could brush my teeth pain-free. The medication had restored my crooked smile. I felt on top of the world, seizing as many opportunities as I could to have a laugh and show off my pearly whites. And Brian made me laugh constantly.

One day, Brian found a can of spam and began to eat it raw out of the tin. The crew fell silent. We looked at each other for a reason why. We stared at him in utter disgust and bewilderment whilst he smiled quietly to himself in his own little world. Just him and his delight over his casual snack. Until he realised we were watching him.

"This isn't a freak show!" he yelled at us.

We exchanged glances in amusement and fell over ourselves in fits of laughter. I had regained my sense of humour by joking around with Brian.

When he was in his room with the door closed, I would call out, "Brian's naked!"

It caught on, and soon the whole crew was doing it.

Sometimes I fantasised about what Brian's athletic body looked like naked. It was hard not to. He was becoming attractive; the more time we spent together. He laughed loudly at my jokes. I was intrigued by the honesty of his expressions as they would change with conversation, allowing me to get to know another part of him that only an observer with a keen eye could admire. I told myself to be careful with my thoughts and not to get too close.

I found a quiet spot to lie down on the sails at the front of the boat to read. Salty fingers stuck to the pages while the sound of *Who Dares Wins* slid through the seawater beneath us. Light sprays misted my olive, sunscreen-covered skin. There had been no wind, the sea calm as my state of mind. We had no choice but to motor, even though we had little fuel left. Lee estimated one day and a half until we arrived in Malta.

I was reading *Memoirs of a Geisha*, after finding a few books on board. It's such a beautiful novel spoken poetically, melodically, and carefully crafted. I enjoyed learning about Japanese culture—respect, stillness, gentle with care. The people seemed so powerful to me. Quiet confidence. All the things I longed for drew me into this culture.

We intercepted travelling insect swarms in the billions, insects that I had not encountered in Australia. Some resembled bees, mosquitoes, dragonflies, and locusts. Lee shared that we were between Tunisia in Africa and Sicily in Italy.

He continued that the locusts were a massive problem in Africa, killing off crops and leaving communities starving. It was indeed a sobering thought that the hard work of millions of people every day, from seed germination, planting, and caring for crops over the seasons, could be destroyed after one visit from a swarm of locusts. I sat watching.

I had lost so much after the rape, but it made me see I was not at risk of losing my life like millions of people in Africa. Our experiences were not comparable, but as I watched a lightning storm off the coast of Sicily, thinking about the uncertainty some communities face, I could see the opportunities that were still available to me; I had control over my *mindset*. I could choose to see myself as a victim, or I could choose to be a survivor. I could stay stuck, break down, and fall apart like the boat seemed to do every day, or I could move forward. Not to forget and not yet ready to forgive, but I could choose to heal. I could choose me.

Brian and I discussed how we came to live in Gibraltar. I had been rebelling my way through Western Europe for three months after leaving London. I was trying to tick off as many "world festivals" from Lonely Planet that I could. On that list was the annual Running of the Bulls festival in Spain, a cultural rite of passage for young men to show their courage. To do so, they must run with the bulls through the streets of Pamplona. The women and children watch, cheering them on. It was very dangerous but exhilarating as a spectator, and the party of a lifetime!

I met Sean on the second day of the festival. With drunk confidence, I approached Sean and his group of friends with a beer bong in hand.

"Take a knee!"

I offered to share my Corona if they would get down onto

one knee and allow me to pour it into a funnel down a hose into their mouth.

Sean, later told me with his usual mark of sarcasm that it was love at first sight.

He and I became friends instantly. He was from Perth, Australia. A year younger. Sean's red hair was where his power resided, and he walked tall like he owned it all. He never skipped a beat and let no one down. Sean liked to tell people he met that he was, in fact, the best looking "ranga" around. I spent most of the festival with Sean and his friends.

After the festival, I had planned to meet up with friends to take a surf trip through Portugal, but it fell through at the last minute because we couldn't contact each other. I accepted that travelling was like that. You had to be flexible, open to a last-minute change of plans, and comfortable with uncertainty. And I thrived on it. Sean turned to me and asked me what I would do if I didn't hear back from them.

"I'm not sure, to be honest."

"Why don't you move to Gibraltar with me?"

I had never heard of this strange place. "Where is it?"

"It's the most southern point of Europe, below Spain, and you can earn the pound there. It's owned by the British."

I looked up to Sean in many ways.

I'm petite, so he would drape his arm on my shoulder and look down at me, with his cute freckles, and say, "Nae, what the fuck are you doing?"

Sean was funny. He just had this intelligence and emotional maturity I hadn't seen in a man my age before. He had this way of calling out my bullshit. Sean made me face my fragility and remedied it with a deep feeling of security. He would watch me question myself and hesitate to make decisions. He could see how I questioned my worth. We clicked; I felt he could see through me. I valued our friendship because he could drag the truth out of me, the fact I was usually hiding from myself. I needed that. I didn't need another person just going with the flow with whatever the fuck I thought I knew about the world or myself.

I needed a friend who would look down at me and say, "Get a fucking grip, Renee, you're better than this. What are you doing with your life? What do you want?"

Then push me to get it. I needed a friend like Sean to teach me about strength and self-assurance. I wanted to find that confidence in myself. I wanted to walk like him, talk like him, and tell people to get a grip like him. I wanted to be the girl version of Sean. I looked up to him.

And that's why I moved to Gibraltar. That and I only had one hundred and fifty pounds left in my wallet and was avoiding returning to London.

~

Brian shared that he had ended up in Gibraltar after finishing sailing the Atlantic Crossing with a lovely couple.

We laughed until we noticed the increase in the wind. At first, it alarmed me, but later on, Lee informed us that if the wind kept up, we would arrive in Malta in two days. Lee told us we would be staying in Malta for three days to work on the boat, restock supplies, and do the touristy thing. My goal was to explore Malta as much as I can.

Brian and I talked about who had been our greatest influencers. I hadn't asked myself that question before.

But almost like a reflex, I heard my mother's advice, "Don't get married and have kids young. Be free and travel."

My mother worked as a flight stewardess in the Australian Air Force. She fell wildly in love with my biological father, who worked as an aviation engineer, and married at eighteen. At twenty, she was pregnant with me. She was the first married woman to be *allowed* to continue working as a flight stewardess in the Air Force.

But when she became pregnant, she knew they would take away her wings and would not allow her to continue to fly. She concealed her pregnancy until, at six months pregnant, her baby bump began to show, and she had no choice but to inform her superiors of the big news. She loved to travel and wanted to do so much more. My mum's biggest regret was not waiting to have children. She wished she would have travelled and experienced her life in more ways than she had.

I could see that she felt starved for what she needed. Never entirely filled up, never overflowing with joy, passion, or vitality. I knew she had had a traumatic childhood which clouded her ability to recognise her self-worth, and I put the puzzle pieces together to realise she had never really experienced great freedom or happiness. Instead, she kept to herself, her heart wrapped up in bandages, because she didn't believe she could trust anyone. It wasn't until her forties that she eventually grew back her butterfly wings and taught herself how to trust again, make friendships, and live life on her terms. My mother inspired my independence.

The stories about Sean and Mum reminded me I too, wanted to feel in control of my life. I valued power, strength, human connection, freedom, and adventure. But most importantly, I appreciated my independence—a path to myself. I didn't have to live out anyone else's dreams.

I could lean into my fragility and answer the hard questions that Brian and Sean both raised. *What the fuck do I want? Do I want to be like Sean? Do I want to make my mother proud? Do I want to be in a relationship with Steve?*

But what I wanted was the wrong question. Instead, I asked myself a better question. *What does my heart need to heal?*

Chapter 6

The glow from the lights of Malta shimmered on the surface of the water in the distance and marked a path for us to follow. The cool breeze aroused the little hairs on my arms to awaken. The helm felt light. One hand managed. The boat rocked back and forth like a ticking clock. I closed my eyes to listen intently to the water as it splashed and fizzled and added another layer to the early emerging composition. Classical music played through the speakers at a low volume, enhancing the song nature had already opened with.

At a distance, the rough cliffs appeared like beautiful old men's cracked faces, the colour of hazelnut and caramel ice cream. I tried to find connections to memories of other places I had seen. I imagined what it might be like to be an ancient explorer, stumbling across a lost world. It looked like a place where the rock monsters might live from *The Never Ending Story*. As we sailed closer, the cliff face began to change into what looked like an old dinosaur resting on its stomach. I wasn't sure if I could make out houses or towns. I saw a palette of colours of natural light browns that blended in with the sharp, rough, rocky landscape. It looked spectacular.

I was intrigued by the idea of Malta. No one on board knew anything about her. She was a mystery to us all. I couldn't wait to find out her secrets. "Who are you, Malta?" I whispered under my breath, my words picked up and carried away with the wind.

I was curious about her magic. I longed for her to whisper her truth in my ear.

"Oh, oh, oh, oh, oh, oh, I want to get close to you, mysterious girl. Move your body close to mine."

The crew looked at me and laughed as I broke into song. I smiled bashfully as I realised I had rudely interrupted Vivaldi's solo.

It suddenly dawned on me. *Am I singing to myself? Is Malta sending me an invitation to get closer to her? But is Malta me? What is happening to me? Where had this depth come from?* It wasn't, "Who are you, Malta?" From now on, it was, "Who are you, Renee?"

It was my own truth that I longed to understand. It was my secrets I needed to unearth. That I needed to get close to.

We arrived in the quiet port of Valetta. It was an enchanting place with motorised gondolas and everything made of stone. The friendly locals spoke English, and they loved to chat, sing loudly, and make jokes.

We befriended a nice couple who owned a bar close by. Lee informed Maria and Patrick of our plans to sail to Phuket. They made us tapas to go with the heavy consumption of alcohol that took place.

It didn't take long before I felt pretty smashed. The oath I swore never to smoke cigarettes again didn't last long. Sorry, God. I was sure I was going to hell. I prayed she was in a forgiving mood.

Two old paedophile-looking men stared eerily at me and all over me. My leg began to twitch. My heart started to race. Sweat boiled onto my forehead. Brian noticed my energy change and looked around the room for the cause. He spotted the men muttering to each other as they refused to redirect their gaze.

"Are you feeling okay? Is it those men?"

"Yeah, it's okay. I might just leave soon. I have to put up with creeps like that all the time. I'm fucking over it," I replied, not wanting to make a scene.

"Well, you don't have to put up with it here." Brian signalled for Patrick's attention behind the bar. "Can you please tell those men over there to stop looking at my girlfriend? They are making her uncomfortable. She just wants a drink in peace. Otherwise, we'll just leave."

"Yeah, I actually noticed them too. Sorry about that," replied Patrick.

Patrick approached the men. They just laughed and continued with the same behaviour until I finished my drink and decided it was too much for me to deal with.

I made eye contact with Patrick. "Thanks for the drinks, and please thank your lovely wife for the tapas. They were delicious."

"Are you leaving? I'll kick those men out if you like."

"No, I don't want any drama. I might just grab a few beers and relax back on the boat. I wouldn't mind some time to myself."

I trusted Malta to keep me safe. I was beginning to believe our songs were the same. I had this feeling that she would watch over me as I walked home that night—my big sister.

After saying goodbye to the crew, I snuck out without the creeps seeing me leave. The rape had messed with my sense of safety, and I only felt truly safe on my own.

As I walked home, aided by the lamp post lights, I stopped to speak to an older man fishing off the pier. "Caught anything?"

"No, but it's not the fish I come out here for," he replied with a genuine smile.

"Oh, really? What do you come out here for?" I laughed, amused.

"Would you like a coffee?" he gestured to his thermos.

I sensed a good story was coming.

"Why not?" I replied as I sat down next to him and dangled my legs off the pier.

Phillipe was sixteen when he fell in love with a girl the same age. They quickly married. She died when she was twenty-three. Philippe explained that everyone was poor back then. So when his wife's kidneys failed, she couldn't get the medical help she needed and died from a heart attack. Phillipe remarried and had been happily married for fifty years.

"I see why you don't come out for the fish."

He smiled back at me. His eyes welled with tears that painted a picture of all the years he had lived without her.

I smiled back. I sensed Phillipe had never quite moved on from his first wife's memory, nor did he wish to. When the moon was at its brightest, he was called to connect with her and all that he remembered her to be, fishing not for the fish but for her in the dark waters of what might have been. This was his time to commune with himself, to connect with his feelings of grief and loss. For the family, they would never have.

Phillipe's story stayed with me as I wept on my walk home. I desperately longed for someone to love me like Phillipe loved his first wife. I doubted Steve loved me like that. I doubted anyone could. I doubted I was even that lovable. It wasn't a man I needed to fish for me in the dark waters. Instead, I needed to dive into the depths of myself and resuscitate the parts that had drowned. There was still time. I had to jump in and stop being afraid of getting wet.

~

Andy, blind drunk, had returned to the boat too. I opted to try out the boat's video camera.

"Why don't you send Peanut a message?" I suggested to Andy with a grin, the camera light on green and facing him ready to film.

"Hello, Peanut. Daddy loves you and misses you! Daddy's in

Malta. Daddy has been sailing for three weeks."

Daddy had too much to drink. I stopped filming him. It didn't feel right, he was too drunk, and I felt like I was taking advantage.

The rest of the crew returned with three visitors whose names I didn't quite catch. Funnily enough, I picked up on their sexual preferences. I was open to exploring my sexuality, preferring to question societies attitudes that told me because I was a woman, I had to be with a man.

The two girls introduced themselves as a couple and the other guy gay. One girl appeared to be hard of hearing. Her friend interpreted what we were saying in sign language. The couple began to get close to me, and one by one, they each kissed me. I wasn't sure what was going on.

The couple ran hyperactively around the deck and jumped on Lee and Nikki, who were trying to make out on the lounge. The couple began kissing each other and then fighting, but it seemed like a bit of an act. I couldn't make sense of their chaotic behaviour. However, I found it rather entertaining, so I filmed them for a short time.

Brian sat next to me. "It was hot watching those girls kiss you. Can I kiss you?" Brian asked, moving towards me.

"No!" I pulled away, uncomfortable.

"If it's about the crew, it could be a secret." The inference repulsed me, triggering memories of what the pedophile neighbour used to say to me.

"Look, I'm just curious about exploring where things might go with the girls, Brian. I'm not interested in anything else." I stood up, feeling disappointed and irritated that he, too, was acting like a creep.

I walked away towards the girls.

"Okay, I'm sorry," Brian apologised sincerely.

"Do you girls want to sleepover in my room?" I offered.

The girls shook their heads. Bizarrely, one girl seemed to have a change of heart and gestured for me to go with her into my room. I looked at her girlfriend for permission, who gave me the nod, signalling it was okay for me to follow her.

I went into my room and closed the door behind me. She kissed me and took off my pants, and started going down on me. I was desensitised from too much alcohol. I thought about just faking an orgasm.

I heard something coming from the hatch. I stuck my head out from underneath the bunk bed and saw her girlfriend and their friend trying to watch.

"No way, you guys are fucked up. What are you doing?" I yelled out to them.

I put my pants on and walked into the galley to find Brian.

"Okay, seriously, Brian. Can you please tell these people to leave? This is getting out of control."

Brian asked them to leave once the girl came out of my room. They listened and left.

The next day, I noticed that my wallet was missing. Lee suggested I must have misplaced it, but I knew it had been stolen. The dramatic performance of our guests the night before made perfect sense now. They created a diversion whilst they stole from us. I had been played like a fool.

But in a somewhat twisted stroke of luck, the girl had left behind her hearing aid. I knew I had leverage because I imagined those devices wouldn't be cheap, and she would have to return for it. I only had one credit card and a bit of money to last me the entire journey home. I had to get my wallet back, and I was quite happy pulling out whatever stops possible to make that happen. If I ran out of money, I would have to borrow from someone on the boat, putting me in a vulnerable position. I didn't want to be indebted to anyone.

I put the hearing aid away somewhere safe while the crew worked on the boat.

I was on a mission to get all chores finished so I could explore Malta. The boys kept disappearing to the bar for beers, and it was slowing us down. I cleaned the inside of the yacht, and Nikki used her networking skills to find a local guy who worked on a water taxi to do our laundry. Nikki also resourcefully had organised with Patrick to drive us to the locations needed to pick up food provisions.

Later that night, Nikki informed me she had seen the couple who I suspected of stealing my wallet at a bar on the marina.

"Thanks, Nikki. You're a legend." I jumped up and kissed her on the cheek, and headed off down the marina puffed up, ready for a fight.

Brian ran after me. "Just be cool, okay. It might be best if I ask them about the wallet."

"I appreciate your help, but I'm okay. I can handle this." I smiled, excited about the impending confrontation.

He held my hand on the way. I loved the way he did that.

I immediately locked eyes with the couple. I greeted them like old friends and sat down.

"Okay, let's not fuck around here. My wallet went missing the same time both of you and your little friend came to visit us on our boat."

"It was our friend. Did you find a hearing aid?" They ratted out their friend with no remorse.

"Yes, I did. But I'm not returning it until my wallet is returned. And if I don't get it back, I'll throw the hearing aid in the harbour." I felt guilty, but this was the only chance I had at ever seeing my wallet again.

"You fucking bitch!" the rat screamed as she threw her chair from under her and stormed off down the marina.

Brian and I headed back to the boat.

"Nice work. You handled that well. I thought you were going to go in there swinging. But you had the hearing aid up your sleeve. I didn't see that coming."

I smiled. Taken over by the heat of the exchange, I turned and kissed Brian. We kissed sweetly in the streets of Malta, and afterwards, we found privacy in my room and each other's arms. I was about to fall asleep when I heard something in the saloon, the living room of the boat. I leapt up to find "the rat" sneaking around in the dark. I was astonished at the girl's nerve.

"Excuse me, what the fuck do you think you're doing? No one invited you on our boat. Get the fuck off, NOW!"

I wanted to grab her hair and unleash my fists on her face. But before I could get anywhere near her, she scampered away up the stairs and down the pier like the filthy vermin she was.

Security called the police after noticing she had boarded the boat without permission. The police returned with the couple and asked about the hearing device. I told them about the situation. They thought I had been reasonable to keep it. The police and the couple left, and an hour later, the police returned with all three of the rats. The police had visited the guy's house where they retrieved my wallet that held my credit card. Not only did the police return all my stolen items, but they also thought I deserved an apology in person from all three of them. The police explained that all three were in on it and had shared my money between them. I cherished the thought that these police officers had taken the time to listen, cared enough to follow up, and to deliver a positive outcome for all involved, especially a teachable moment to the posse of rats.

I returned the hearing aid and gave the police a big hug and thanked them.

Brian and I went back to bed and, like we had originally intended, made love with little concern for the nights ahead. I was smitten by Brian the first time he held my hand when we were in Sardinia on the way to the hospital. Support had become my aphrodisiac—someone who could show up in the most stressful of situations. I felt I owed him so much. I repaid Brian in the only way I knew how to repay a man, by sharing the only thing I thought they valued about me. My body.

"Thank you so much for all your support. You have no idea what that means to me," I whispered to him.

But FUCK! What about Steve? I felt guilty.

I was supposed to be coming home for Steve. I wanted to avoid complications. *What was I thinking?*

I had high hopes and dreams for a future with Steve. I reassured myself that Steve would understand when I was ready to tell him what had happened. I decided not to overthink it and to just live in the moment. I knew it was wrong, ethically, and morally. But it also felt so very right. I wasn't technically cheating on Steve because I wasn't technically in a relationship with Steve yet. It was all going to become official when we were reunited.

I told the crew about the recovery of my stolen wallet in the morning. No one could believe it. I knew my instincts were right. I just had to trust myself.

~

Nikki and I, desperate to explore, snuck off to go on a quick motorboat tour of Valetta. We wanted to experience Malta, not just visit bars. Lee felt the need to control everything the crew did at the port. I understood it was his responsibility and priority to complete the delivery. This included overseeing all provisioning, cleaning, and jobs at each stop. But we couldn't do anything without his permission. I didn't sign up to have no free time. The crew deserved to rest and enjoy their time in their own way.

When we mentioned we wanted to do some sight-seeing, he shrugged off our requests with, "We will see if we have time after all the tasks are complete."

After returning to the boat, I felt slightly awkward every time I walked past Brian. I felt a need to touch him, but I knew I shouldn't. The night prior was not just a drunken mistake. It was something we had both felt for each other and acted on. *Go for it*, I decided.

We kissed as we passed each other. Carpe diem - Seize the fucking day.

Step 3. Choose Your Song

"Wild Women dance to the beat of their own drum."

SHIKOBA

Chapter 7

It was great to be back at sea with no problems; no thieves, no creepy men, no drunken disorderly behaviour, no hangovers, no sleepless nights, no chaos, no alcohol. You would think it would be tougher living at sea than on land, but it felt quite the opposite to me. The world seemed safer on a sailing boat. The water wrapped me up in cotton wool, keeping me from harm. The boat was becoming my cocoon. I started to realise that the person I needed protection from the most was perhaps myself. I couldn't hurt myself at sea. *But why did I want to hurt myself?*

The rape wasn't my fault. I didn't rape myself. I contemplated the support Brian offered me. Which was the care I needed to provide to myself. Then I wouldn't feel obligated to fuck someone for it.

Brian had no idea what had happened to me. He had no idea what truths tormented my mind. I wanted to keep it that way. Brian was this sailing Superhero out of a Hollywood blockbuster, and my stuff was too real. I could still pretend I was in the romantic part of the movie when I was with Brian.

He and I had been enjoying getting to know one another physically, my beer belly had disappeared, and I began to feel supercharged with sexual energy. We seized every opportunity to release the tension. We made love helming under the moonlight and at dawn when everyone was asleep. It felt naughty, and that's what I loved about it. During the day, we made love in my room.

I worried we might be intruding on Nikki's space too. It was a bunk bed, after all. I discussed my concerns with Nikki. "What could we do to make things a bit more comfortable for you to access the room when we were together?"

"Yeah, you're right. It is a little awkward. Why don't we both just hang sarongs over our bunk beds, then we both have privacy?"

It had been sweltering and uncomfortable sharing a single bed with Brian. We agreed to stop doing sleepovers. Brian moved back to his bunk at night, and I slept in the saloon. That way, we could both get a good night's sleep.

From time to time, Brian would fall asleep in the cockpit after working hard on a mechanical repair. It was usually when everyone was asleep and the night was still. I would drift off into my head, and my heart would start remembering. My heart would start hurting. As I yearned for the place I called "home."

For the people I had left behind. For my family. For my friends. For the people who still gave a fuck about me.

I found when I left Australia, the friends I went to school with just dropped out of the picture. The girls who slept in Bree's room, who laughed at my back-to-front jeans. No messages, no emails, no likes, no nothing. WTF. I wondered if it was because they found out about the rape and blamed me. And it hurt me deeply. Another loss. It made me angry. I had dreams where I told them how hurt I felt that they had just stopped caring about me. I began to question whether those friendships were even true friendships in the first place, but it hurt nonetheless. I tried to tell myself that with loss also comes gain. The time away made space for other friendships to blossom.

I daydreamed for hours about the comfort of my old bedroom.

"Your little haven," as Mum lovingly referred to it.

The walls painted bright pink and green. My art on display

and my guitar waiting for me in the corner. I realised, I hadn't created anything since the rape and being away from home. I had left behind my creativity right next to my self-respect in the room I last grieved in.

I imagined being back in my room with my mum sitting on my veranda, sipping chai tea, and playing the guitar with the kookaburras singing in the background.

My youngest brother Jake was fourteen. I really wanted to see him experience adolescence. I remembered him crying at the departure gates of Sydney airport as I left for my travels. We hugged, and for the first time, I became aware of how much he loved me and how much I was going to miss him. I adored him with all my heart. But I somehow missed the part where I felt important to him. I'm certain it was always there, but I never thought about what I meant to anyone else before like I did in that one moment. It was the most precious goodbye gift he could have possibly given me. A hug and the wisdom that I was indeed loved, very much important, and I wasn't a completely worthless piece of shit, something I had never felt before until after the rape. As I watched the tears stream down his face, I wanted nothing more than to wipe them away and take away his sadness.

I had two brothers. Tim was twenty and planned to travel too. I was looking forward to returning home and catching up with him before he left. He was keen to spread his wings and see the world. Tim was gifted in everything he put his mind to, especially anything to do with the water. He could surf, snowboard, and loved fishing. He would probably love sailing, too, if he tried it. I was certain he wouldn't be home for quite some time. I wondered when all the family would be able to sit around the table together, with the smell of steak and sausages on the barbeque and the taste of a cold beer.

To take my mind off home, I relaxed on the deck and dangled

my legs off the bow. I watched dolphins surfing the bow wave just a metre below my hand as I attempted to reach out to touch them.

~

I started to notice a cockroach infestation on the boat. I saw them everywhere. What concerned me most was that they were crawling on the cooker and benchtops. Everything was spotless, and we never left food out. Lee told us they lived in the bilges, and it costs a lot of money to have a yacht sprayed with pesticide. He told us a story about some pest control guys who came out to a boat he had worked on in Thailand. They taped up all the cracks to avoid potential leaks. What they didn't realise was when all the hatches are closed properly, yachts are already airtight.

Last night, I jumped out of my bed as fast as a lightning bolt. I switched the light on and pulled down my pants. Brian and I had broken our no sleepover rule. My abrupt movement startled him; he had no idea what I was doing.

"There's a fucking cockroach in my undies!" I blurted out.

"What? Turn the light off. You've got the creepy crawlies again. Go back to sleep. You've got cockroach paranoia."

I didn't see any cockroaches in my undies, but I swear I felt something there. I was grateful I always wore underwear. I got straight up and sprayed the room with cockroach spray. Maybe Brian was right, and perhaps I was getting creeped out. The past few days, I felt like my skin was crawling every time I laid down. I hated insects, and I could spot them scuttling around anywhere. I was so glad I slept with earplugs. I read this crazy story a few years back about a cockroach crawling into a guy's ear in prison. It laid eggs which turned into maggots and his ear had to be sliced with a razor. I needed the cockroaches to fuck off so I could try to relax.

~

On the eighteenth day, there was a fair bit of swell, but a good wind blew. We needed the wind to keep up the speed to make good time arriving in Port Said.

With our approach to Egypt, Lee told us stories about the Suez Canal and bribery. I hadn't even heard of the Suez Canal before. He told us sailing down the Suez Canal would make us feel like we were on a toy boat compared to the big daddy transformer ships out there.

My biological father had worked abroad in Saudi Arabia for ten years. I would never have imagined I would be so close to Saudi Arabia. He refused to let me visit him because he told me it was a stringent Muslim country. "It was no place for a girl like you, Renee."

What the fuck does that mean, Dad? I wondered.

"It's not safe for Western girls with big mouths. You won't be respected there. In Saudi Arabia, there is no such thing as freedom of speech like in Australia, and you could get into big trouble there. Renee, I heard they cut off your hand if you don't do your homework. No, you're not visiting."

Whether or not the information was correct, I dropped the issue and never asked to visit again. It was my father's stories that created trepidation in approaching a predominantly Muslim country.

Suddenly, the helm broke. It sounded like a bone-breaking— a huge crack or a snapping sound. The helm started spinning, and so did the yacht. Brian was mid-sentence when it happened, but he dove into action-man mode, straight out of the cockpit to bring down the sails.

"Lee, helm's gone!" he called out.

"Fuck!" Lee screamed back in sheer frustration.

He bolted on deck straight from his sleep. He felt the helm and immediately brought the sails down. All I could do was sit, be quiet, and stay safely secured to the yacht whilst Brian and Lee figured out what to do next. I felt powerless, especially as the wind and the waves beat the boat.

The boys worked fast and efficiently to stabilise the situation. We turned the spotter lights on so passing ships could see us in the distance. We were sitting ducks in the ocean. No motor, sails, or helm meant we weren't going anywhere.

Lee instructed Nikki to watch the monitor for ships from one in the morning until first light. If anything came even remotely close on the radar, she was instructed to wake Lee to assess and, if necessary, radio the other ship to inform them of our situation so they could divert their course. Luckily, Nikki only needed to wake Lee once to radio a ship during the night. The helm was only kept going by two screwdrivers stuck between two silver plates as wedges and enforced against something else. I don't understand mechanics; truthfully, I'm not interested in learning much about it. I was okay with having no idea what was happening when things broke down.

I realised that was my old avoidance pattern emerging again. I didn't understand the rape experience, which lulled me into avoiding learning about the pain it caused and look how that worked out. My body began to break down! This boat was starting to resemble my body. It was teaching me the importance of taking care of my vessel.

Brian and I slept in the saloon because the boat was being tossed around all night. I imagined this is what it would feel like in a washing machine on the full wash cycle. It was dark, rocky, and frightening. The stars looked like fireflies, buzzing and zigzagging in the sky. It made me dizzy and nauseous.

Something I can only explain as spiritual had been moving within me. Everything that was happening felt like it had so much more meaning than what I was used to noticing. I prayed every night before sleep. Praying for wind, for good weather, for the safety of the crew, and for people back home.

If you had asked me about religion or spirituality before I came onto *Who Dares Wins*, I would have probably said that it was great for hope but had more negatives than positives, like dividing people and causing conflict. However, since being at sea, I had developed an appreciation for the power of prayer and intention.

Every single time I would pray, something compelling would happen. I felt like I was being rewarded when my prayers were answered. It felt like I had someone watching my back, keeping me safe. Whatever it was seemed to have some serious pull with Mother Nature because she appeared to back off whenever I asked for it.

Lee had been in a shitty mood for days. I knew there had been a lot of issues with the boat. Also, he blamed Nikki and me for not getting enough provisions. I was becoming increasingly tired of the sarcastic commentary he directed towards us. It would really serve Lee well as a leader if he would change his attitude, cut us some slack, and choose to focus on what we were doing right instead of what we were doing wrong. It was difficult to forecast food consumption patterns based on people we hardly know. Plus, we had no prior experience in provisioning. Maybe if he wasn't so consumed by controlling our every move and drinking beers instead of actually focusing on the important responsibilities, like overseeing provision plans, we would have had a little more guidance and wouldn't have disappointed him. It was definitely an area we needed to improve as a team, and I took responsibility and learned from it.

I avoided him by staying in my cabin unless it was my watch. It felt like I was walking on eggshells around him. It took me back to childhood memories of my step-father. He could be nice one minute and then turn into a complete asshole the next. I never really knew where I stood when he was in one of those moods, and it fucked with my head. I had that same feeling of being powerless and wanting to escape. I read to take my mind off things.

One day, the boys were trimming the sails and asked me to helm. The sails were almost going overboard as they tried to pull them down on the starboard side. I could see Lee and Nikki stumbling on deck as the boat was tipping from port to starboard. I was doing my best to keep on course and keep the vessel as steady as possible. I must have been distracted by all the commotion on deck.

I looked outwards and noticed a fucking huge tanker. Lee looked out at the same time and yelled, "Did anyone see that ship?"

Everyone replied, "No!"

"I did, but I thought it was the ship that passed us earlier," I responded, believing honesty was the best policy.

"Fuck!" he replied.

He tried to start the engine. It stalled three times but eventually started, and he helped us out of the boat's path. I could see both port and starboard lights, and it was coming straight towards us about three hundred metres away.

I imagined the worst possible scenarios. *What if we smashed into it? All of us could have been seriously injured or died. It would be my fault because it was my responsibility to be on watch.* I also imagined Lee might literally kill me and throw me overboard for the near-miss; he might never trust me to helm again or, even worse, kick me off the boat at the next stop.

Fuck! I was angry at myself.

I trembled with fright for an hour. I felt like everyone could see my nervous tension. It was as if I was on a scary ride, and I wanted to scream out to the attendant to stop the ride and let me off.

About half-hour after, Lee asked if I would like to helm again. I felt like a child who had just had the confidence knocked out of them. I knew I had to get back up. I continued to tremble for some time, but I focused on my breathing. Eventually, my heartbeat returned to normal, and the trembling stopped. I knew I had to take this opportunity to rebuild trust in myself again.

I cried as I rehashed the frightening experience with Brian later that day. Brian smiled and pulled me in close under his arm.

"We missed the transport ship easily. We weren't even on course with the ship at all. Lee reacted dramatically. It was fine," he assured me.

I wasn't sure if that was true or not, but Brian eased my mind after a great lesson learnt. I decided I would always watch the horizon closely from now on and call out if I saw anything that looked remotely dangerous.

Brian's positive, supportive words were so very soothing. None of the crew had the same positive attitude. Even after all the day's drama, he still had a massive smile on his face. He loved all the action. I found it terrifying and exhausting. But he definitely did his best to help me sleep that night.

Chapter 8

On the twentieth day, the weather had been quite erratic. The sun was intensifying by the day, not to mention the long list of problems needing repairs. I looked forward to the mornings. Brian woke me with news the swell had dropped off. I preferred not to feel scared out of my wits every second day.

To combat the sun, we created a makeshift shade house over the cockpit. The shade was a welcome reprieve after having no protection for four weeks on deck.

Besides the weather, the mechanical complications were coming hard and fast. In just a few days, the prop shaft coupling broke (the bit that connects the engine to the propeller which means no propeller), the alternator disconnected itself (which meant no electricity, and if the engine wasn't running, we wouldn't have any power on the boat), there was a fuel problem with the pipelines, and a rope wrapped around the propeller.

By this point, the delays no longer concerned me. I was letting go of any disappointment to do with the estimated arrival dates. I was learning to trust that Brian and Lee had all the skills necessary to take care of it. But I was becoming increasingly concerned about Lee's growing frustrations. And if Lee was stressed, his mood impacted the entire crew.

We had fourteen hours until we arrived at Port Said. Lee wanted to avoid arriving in the dark; he said it would be too dangerous. We slowly made our way toward the port, zigzagging with little care to stay on course and by pulling down the sails. To kill time, Lee suggested swimming off the back of the yacht. For curiosity's sake, I checked the depth gauge—the water was fifty-seven metres deep, roughly the same height as the Sydney Harbour Bridge from sea level to its base. We trailed a rope from the boat that was attached to a fender that looked like a balloon. Lee explained that a boat is never still in the water, so it was important for each of us to stay with the boat by hanging onto the rope as it trailed behind.

Nikki, with no hesitation, dived straight in with perfect form. Brian did a huge bomb, and I cautiously slid myself down the stairs. Andy, by choice, positioned himself on shark watch.

Nikki was in her element, cackling loudly as she leapt from the highest point she could into the crystal clear water. This was her favourite pastime at day parties in the marina in Gibraltar. I loved seeing her cheerful smile; it radiated like a lighthouse, letting you know it was safe to approach with happiness too. I hadn't seen her so happy since we left.

Brian, with fluorescent green goggles, held his breath for the longest time to check underneath the boat to clean off any barnacles.

I sat on the ladder, reluctant to let go as I contemplated my insignificance in the world. I pondered the depth of the water and felt quite nervous about potential sharks that might mistake me for something else. I clung to the ladder tightly, clinging to the very idea of my self-importance. I was trying to rediscover my confidence and trust in myself, and these thoughts were not helping.

After a short time, with no help from Brian, I let go. I focused on slowing my breath. I trusted in my ability as a strong swimmer. It was easier than I thought to swim alongside the rope. And when I needed a break, I could just reach out with one hand, find the rope, and allow the boat to pull me along smoothly through the water as I lay on my back staring up at the limitless blue sky.

A pod of dolphins came over to check us out. I tried to dive under the water, curious whether they were close enough to see them playing. Underwater, they appeared much closer, misleading me to think I would have any chance of connecting with one by touch. I chuckled to myself as they toyed a slow game of hide-and-go-seek.

~

The night prior, as we approached Port Said, countless boats lined the horizon. We had a couple of ships pass quite closely but nothing alarming. We woke Lee when we arrived at the Suez Canal entry point at five-thirty am. We brought the sails down and entered.

It cost two thousand three hundred US dollars to travel through the Suez Canal with a pilot. It was compulsory to have a pilot on board. Talk about a monopoly. I'm sure it was costly to carve up the land to create an artificial sea-level waterway in Egypt connecting the Mediterranean Sea with the Red Sea. It offered watercraft a shorter journey between the Northern Atlantic and Southern Indian Ocean. Its length is one-hundred and ninety-three kilometres, and it saves seafarers seven-thousand kilometres in travel time. It is no Sydney Harbour tunnel toll fee, that's for sure.

The driver of the motorboat that delivered the pilot tried to bribe the crew with cigarettes. Still, our pilot didn't seem fixed on it, so it wasn't acknowledged. He directed us into the berth next to a large cruise boat.

The Egyptians who worked on it seemed friendly, offering cigarettes and a red tea that you mix with sugar. It tasted like dirt, but I drank it anyway and thanked them for their hospitality.

We got our hands on some beer, and we smashed them down

as fast as we could. But when they ran out, that was it. I felt frustrated that we couldn't go anywhere because visas cost twenty-five US, and it was Ramadan, which meant that nothing was open.

I went for a walk with the crew; we saw a few people, tables and chairs, and fences—nothing else. I felt like a prisoner. I tried to imagine what it must feel like to be an asylum seeker waiting to be processed in detention centres living behind fences like this. I watched the people outside from inside the fence. I felt trapped in a place I didn't wish to be with people I wouldn't mind a break from, and I longed for comforts that only life on land could offer that would ease my nostalgia for home.

Prayer music echoed off the dusty walls of the concrete buildings that lined the streets. The women were dressed conservatively, fully covered from head to toe with a hijab. I was wearing a singlet and a long skirt. I immediately knew my lack of clothing could be interpreted as a great sign of cultural disrespect. We watched for a few moments and returned to the boat.

I had grown up in a family that believed the nonsense Australian media corporations spewed up to profit from inventing hate and fear through the production of negative stereotypes. I was raised in a society that taught me that Muslim women were oppressed. Therefore, I should hate and fear Muslim men. I grew up in a predominantly white community with one student from Pakistan in our school of 1,200 students. London was the first time I had ever met a person who believed in Islam. His name was Anas.

I was curious about people who had different beliefs from me. I discovered it was only through developing a friendship with Anas that all the labels around the Muslim stereotype started to fall away. I began to see Anas as a person instead of defining him by his beliefs. Not that his beliefs ever posed a threat to me anyway. I quickly realised the engrained racism was all an illusion created to separate and divide us from learning, understanding, and discovering true compassion and connection amongst humanity.

On my first encounter meeting the pilot who escorted us down the Suez Canal, he asked if I was married.

I should have said yes, but I said, "No."

He showed me photos of his family and asked me for my bracelet. I thought he just wanted to have a look at it. He asked me if I would like to marry his son. I laughed it off and told him I had to marry an Australian boy.

He kept looking at my feet. I kept my legs covered, but it was too hot to wear shoes.

Lee asked the pilot a question, and he answered, but Lee didn't understand him. I repeated the pilot's response to Lee. The pilot gestured with one finger to his lips, an internationally recognised symbol to silence someone. He gestured he would only answer Lee.

I interpreted his gesture as confirmation that Muslim men oppress women, and I felt like the pilot was expressing sentiments that women should be seen and not heard. My stomach turned to stone with anger. This cultural difference that men do the talking, and women should trust in the men to lead and take care of them just didn't sit well with me.

I was only starting to learn how to trust the men in the crew to safely get us home —I would not allow myself to trust a man to take care of me for the rest of my life. That idea was completely foreign and inconceivable, but I languished in the shallows at the possibility of discovering I could trust like that and surrender all control to the support of another human being. I had to find that trust in myself first.

The pilot insisted on my bracelet. He wanted to exchange

souvenirs.

"My friend gave it to me, and I'm not giving it to anyone," I responded with blunt force brushing away a fly from my face.

"We are friends, and God likes it when we exchange items," he insisted.

"No, sorry." I lit up a cigarette and again brushed several flies that were irritating me. I needed an Australian cork hat to deal with the flies.

"You know, it's Ramadan, women no smoking."

Fuck this guy. I continued to smoke until I finished my cigarette.

We tried our best to be respectful by consuming our meals out of his sight in the galley. I stood up without saying another word and moved to the front of the boat away from him.

I tried to calm myself by taking in a deep breath, but I coughed on the smell of camel shit and ash from burning fires. I turned my head to the left, looking out over sand dunes, and to the right, green palm trees and fishermen. Tents lined the canal fisherman used for rest breaks when the sun was scorching, spread out amongst intimidating men in khaki-coloured camouflage, holding guns. There were many rowboats with bed sheets as sails powered by small, thin men with wrinkled copper skin fishing with nets that refused to move when huge tankers one thousand times their size approached them. The guards and fisherman wolf-whistled and waved to us with big smiles on their faces. I smiled back.

My anger subsided as I started to understand their actions were not intended to make me feel uncomfortable but were the actions of people who did not know this behaviour was considered offensive to women in the Western culture. As I acknowledged my lack of knowledge, I found tolerance for unwanted attention for the time being.

To save money paying for a berth, we anchored at our stop. Again, we couldn't purchase visas because of everything being closed for Ramadan. I wasn't a happy camper. I missed civilisation and the simple things like chocolate, alcohol, washing clothes, hot showers, going out for dinner, chatting with a complete stranger, and buying something from a corner store. I felt like I was stuck somewhere in the middle. I wasn't at sea, and I wasn't on land.

Lee's way of helping the crew cope with the frustration is to get them stoned. *Fuck it.*

The crew accepted his help. Brian and I laid on the deck with our eyes closed, listening to the serene prayer music emanating from all directions. I could hear children's laughter, car horns, a game of some sort, an umpire blowing his whistle every so often. I was comforted by the sounds of the real world yet disturbed by knowing I wasn't a part of it. I was officially a fringe dweller— that feeling of not belonging anywhere now felt like a true lived experience. I wondered what my friends and family were doing.

We continued down the Suez Canal the next day, running aground as we docked along the jetty of a yacht club at Suez. Numerous men ran down to the boat, offering their services. After the exorbitant laundry expenses in Malta, we did our washing in the yacht club bathroom sink. We suspected our visas would take a lifetime to arrive and figured it would keep us productive whilst we passed the time. Without visas, the crew was restricted to the decrepit grounds of the yacht club, which featured a toilet block, some chairs and tables, a tiny kiosk that only sold soft drinks, and a children's playground that resembled the Chernobyl disaster aftermath.

Brian and I amused ourselves on the playground for a short time. We played on horse-shaped swings. The paint was peeling, and Brian's horse had two missing legs.

The crew was ready for bed by nine-pm. The patience waiting for beer ran dry. The guide returned at nine-forty-five pm just when Brian and I were about to go to bed. Brian bounced up the hatch to find out he couldn't buy any. He was not a happy camper. No one was. We settled in for sleep again when several men came running down the jetty towards our boat. They were immigration people with our passports and visas.

"Yes! We're free!"

Nikki, Brian, Andy, and I sprinted out of the yacht club immediately on a mission to find beer. But first, we needed to withdraw money. We followed a bank sign down a street, which ended up being dominated by street kids and women wearing black head-to-toe dresses with only openings for their eyes, forcefully begging for money.

"Madam, please, one pound!"

I wish I could have spared some money, but I would have been lucky if what I had left would be enough for myself. We turned back and power-walked along the main road until we reached a busy area with shisha tents. They all looked dirty. I could see elderly men staring ominously out at us as they toked away at their shisha pipes; we knew we stood out as tourists.

We asked a few locals on the way back where we could find a bar. We understood and respected it was Ramadan, but we couldn't accept that there was absolutely no alcohol on offer to foreigners. We were directed to an international hotel. The bar sold beer! We were so happy. After all the drama changing currencies, we could relax. The bar attendant chewed on a large piece of hashish as he served us our hard-earned cold beverages. The bar was dull and lacked any ambiance, but we couldn't complain considering our limited options.

I was fairly drunk after five pints of Egyptian Stella. Feeling frisky, Brian and I headed back to my room on the boat. That led to rough, playful sex. My teeth grazed his neck as he pushed my cheek against the wall. I slapped him whenever he crossed my pain threshold. We were two consenting adults, having fun and letting off some steam.

He pushed my back up against the mirror, and I slapped his face. Brian growled with a mischievous grin that let me know we were fooling around. I yearned for him. And I could tell he desired me by the way he bit his lip in the reflection of the fogged-up mirror. We tore each other's clothes off—my legs around his waist. Our eyes locked. Those piercing eyes. Eyes for days. That feeling. Ecstasy. Lost. Found. Sweat. Energy. Heat. Wet. Slippery. Scintillation. A creative expression. A rhythm. A humming. We were making music. And what a sensual song it was.

Chapter 9

I looked at Brian with dreamy eyes as my leg draped over his. He was still sleeping. It was hot, but I wanted to press repeat on the song we made last night. *Damn. He got me.*

But then the regret started to pour over my naked body like a bad drum solo that left me feeling dirty and unclean. The shame began to take form. I knew what I was doing wasn't right. I wasn't honest with myself. I was falling in love with Brian.

I wasn't the same person that left Gibraltar. I needed to talk to Steve. I wanted to continue exploring this relationship with Brian, but I needed to discuss my insights with Steve. I didn't need his permission. I needed to tell him how I had changed. I was starting to understand that my running track record involved chasing anything or anyone who could lift me out of my reality and could support me emotionally at the same time. Not that there was anything wrong with that either. Everybody does that in some way. But I wanted something more tangible. Something that would last.

Why is my love so contextual? Why is my love dependent on a place to connect to it? Am I changing that quickly that my relationships never stood the test of time with travel?

As much as it hurt to admit it, this meant I was inevitably going to break hearts on the way. Not intentionally. I was a lover, not a destroyer of dreams. But I was also a seeker. And I refused to cage the part of me that wanted to experience more.

The fact was, I had replaced Steve with Brian. I was chasing moments like the night before to numb myself or perhaps feel more. Still, I would never find my way back home if I kept deviating from the path. The relationships external to the one I had with myself were uncertain, which left too much to chance. The relationships I sought out always led to losing myself in the quick, easy fixes, and intensity they offered.

Giving up Brian was all too immediate and something I was not prepared to do because I felt like I needed him more than I had ever needed anyone for survival. But I could choose to uncomplicate things for everyone involved. I needed to make some changes to this pattern. I wasn't sure how yet, but I had to start by talking about it with Steve. He deserved to know where he stood and where my head was. This situation felt all too familiar.

The new owner of *Who Dares Wins* had organised a local guide to take the crew on a day trip to Cairo. The guide waited for us outside the yacht club. We flashed our passports to immigration like FBI agents investigating a crime as we passed through the gates to freedom. On the highway to Cairo, I noticed lines painted on the roads indicating lanes but driving between the lanes mustn't have been enforced as drivers ignored the visual directive. They just drove wherever the fuck they felt like, even in the shoulder lane.

I was tired, so I napped on the way, looking out the window now and again at the desert landscape.

We made our way over to see the Sphinx and the Pyramids. The driver stopped in the middle of the bridge that crossed the river Nile for us to take photos and film. I pinched myself, wiping dust off my skin just to make sure I wasn't dreaming.

I tried to imagine what it would be like to travel back to ancient Egyptian times. I tried to remember what I learned at school in history class. Nothing. So many years spent learning and studying, and I hadn't retained an ounce of information.

We haggled with an Egyptian man to ride camels and horses to see the Pyramids and Sphinx through the Sahara Desert. At first, he said fifty Egyptian pounds for forty-five minutes, but we bartered with him to lower the price. Once we agreed on a price, we mounted our camels. We ended up having to pay fifty for the ride and fifty for entry into the Pyramid area. *Fuck it.* We paid for it.

Haggling, or bartering, was a constant sore point for me travelling. It shits me to almost tears. They tell you what you want to hear, then try to rip you off at the last minute. This bothered me more since the rape, as I had developed fear around being taken advantage of, even extending to my finances.

The local men tied sarongs in the shape of turbans and placed them on our heads. Dripping in sweat, we set off riding through the Sahara Desert towards the pyramids. It felt like I was an archaeologist about to explore the pyramids for the first time in one of *The Mummy* movies.

Nikki and Andy were on horses trotting downhill. Brian performed his best interpretation of "Lawrence of Arabia" with his camel galloping off in the distance. Astonished, I started to laugh. *Where did he learn to ride a camel?*

He looked as though he had been riding camels for years. His white headscarf flowed behind him in the breeze. He looked sexier than ever. I was convinced Brian was related to Bear Grylls. I was in awe of his fearlessness and felt lucky to be with such a remarkable man.

We entered the temple and viewed the Sphinx. It was much smaller than I imagined, but I was astounded by the magnificence of the Pyramids. We could see them from miles away. Whilst we were driving towards Cairo, I looked up to see the Pyramids towering over everything else as if God herself had made them.

The enormous amount of work it would take to build these structures to the size they stood blew my mind.

The driver took us to the token tourist shops. I wanted to explore a local bazaar street market, but instead the guide drove us to his friends' shops.

It took nearly two hours to get back to Suez from Cairo, and we passed two overturned trucks on the way. I tried to sleep and not look at the road ahead. Nikki, Brian, and I all rested on each other like little kids after a big day out.

We then had a sleep and went for a couple of beers at a place called Summer Palace. At ten pm, Brian, Nikki, Andy, and I caught a local bus, which was a minivan with no doors, into town. The rule was it could pick up and drop off passengers anywhere along the main road. We hopped off in the town centre. Dozens of crowded streets lined with market stalls.

I was interested to know why women in Cairo appeared to dress to Western standards wearing jeans and a tight shirt with a hijab. Still, in Suez, it was very conservative. I was informed Islamic culture was much more traditional in smaller towns like Suez compared to big cities like Cairo, where fashion was embraced by the city youth.

We asked at a stall for the internet, and they told us they had it. They tried to sell us everything but then gave us drinks for free, and told us the internet had been down for four days. I didn't understand the contradictions. I wanted to email Steve. We kept searching for an internet café with no luck.

We explored the streets for a while with Nikki and Andy. They headed back to Summer Palace. Brian and I wanted to continue exploring. I enjoyed being amongst the culture and the people rather than sitting in a bar getting pissed with people I had just spent twenty-four hours a day with for the past month. I wanted some space from the crew before I had to board the boat again to leave for Djibouti in South Africa, which would take eight to twelve days.

Brian and I met Fazi, a local guy. Fazi used to work as a tour guide and spoke perfect English. He had married a Dutch girl and lived in Holland for many years. We asked where we could find a shisha bar. Fazi told us the bars around there were street bars and not for us. He was waiting for his friend to pick him up to go to a nice area with comfortable places, and he invited us to join them.

The area was nice and near the waterfront. Fazi took us to his friend's shisha bar. I had to go to the bathroom, and Fazi insisted to the shisha bar owner that the toilets must be cleaned before I used them. There was no toilet door, only a flag covering the doorway. Brian kept watching for other people while I went.

There were only men in the shisha bars. As usual, all the men ogled at me. We were the only tourists. The shisha bar owner wouldn't let me do a thing. I went to pull a cigarette from my packet only to immediately have one in my hand and lit before I could even move. It was hilarious. I wasn't used to VIP treatment where I came from.

The owner was twenty-three years old. He paid a lot of attention to me, even though he couldn't speak a word of English. Maybe because I wore less clothing than girls he was used to seeing. Maybe he was intrigued by the idea of "the foreigner," or perhaps he just thought I was rich. I didn't understand what was so interesting about me as a Westerner.

The owner insisted I take a copy of one of his modelling photos. He demanded his friends take pictures on their phones while he posed next to me. The owner was jumping around excited like a love-sick schoolboy.

Fazi made fun of him. "If I had a hose, I'd hose you down, asshole."

I was amused as Fazi called all of his friends "assholes," and they didn't seem to mind.

The owner offered me a joint and insisted I smoked most of it. I shared it with his friends. He made me a cappuccino and wrote his name in chocolate on top. All the attention was flattering but very strange. Brian found it entertaining that in a matter of moments, I was no longer a human being but a mythical creature from a faraway land worthy of photographic proof of such a wild encounter.

Fazi introduced another friend, who was a club DJ. He was mixing tunes on his laptop. Brian and I were smoking and dancing when the giggles started kicking in. It cost us four US for our night at the shisha bar.

We thanked everyone for their hospitality, generosity, and kindness.

In the taxi on the way back to port, Brian asked me about Anas. "Hey, you said your friend Anas was Muslim. Tell me more about him."

"I wouldn't say Anas was culturally different to me at all besides praying to Allah, which he hardly ever spoke about. He was half Malaysian and English and had lived most of his life in England. He referred to himself as a bad Muslim because he drank just as much as me. I met Anas after Steve moved home. We were close friends for about six months until the edges started to blur."

"Oh, really? You were more than friends? Was it hard for you to move on after Steve?"

"Yes, it was. I was quite happy with the friendship, but I also didn't understand boundaries. I invited Anas to sleep over and stay in my bed because I didn't want to be alone, and I enjoyed his company so much. I also wanted a cuddle. I didn't want a boyfriend, but I knew sleepovers sent the wrong message."

But why? Why can't I have a friend sleep over, but there is no sex? Who invented these fucking rules?

"I guess it's not fair when one person wants more than the other person. I used to cry sometimes at night about how much I missed Steve. Anas provided emotional support, and somehow the lines got blurred. My Australian friends badgered me to be with Anas. They wanted to see Anas happy and in love, you know, to get the girl. I don't know; I just went with it. Anas was special to me, so I guess I just gave him what he wanted."

"Yeah, I get that. You don't have to be with a guy just because that's what they want."

"I didn't get that at the time. I was used to men wearing me down until I gave in to what they wanted. I never just sat down and thought, 'Hey, Renee, what do you want? Will this nurture you?' I just relied on the external advice of everyone else. I was happy pleasing everyone else. If it made them happy, I would do it. I never thought about the consequence of trying to please everyone else and not myself. But you know what I've learnt happens when you live like that? You end up disappointing everyone around you because it was never right for you. It's impossible to make everyone else happy."

"Is that what happened? Did you end up disappointing Anas?"

"Worse. I broke his heart. Just like I'm about to break Steve's when we find a fucking internet connection. Anas was an extraordinary person to me. He really gave me this gift of loving me in a way I had never experienced. It scared the hell out of me. I found it very difficult to receive. I felt overwhelmed by it. He did nothing wrong. He was so kind to me. He would deliver get-well-soon packs when I was sick without being asked. He would organise these fun cricket days out in Hyde Park with all our friends. He took me away on lovely weekends in the countryside.

He would take me out for dinner. He loved to show me all the great places to see in London. He made my London experience the best it could be, and I was so grateful.

"I guess, giving him what he wanted from me seemed to be how I showed him my gratitude. But deep down, I only wanted friendship. But I didn't want to let him go either. I wanted to continue this fun way of life, and I didn't want to hurt him. I thought I broke it off when I left London to travel in Europe, but he came to visit me in Amsterdam. I let him. I missed him. I didn't sleep with him. I thought he knew we weren't together. But then he came to visit me in Venice, and I had changed. I had grown more confident. I still missed my friend, though, so I let him come to Venice. When he arrived in Venice, I wanted to really make certain he knew we were just friends. But he refused to accept that. It was devastating to watch him drink himself into a stupor over those four days. We walked through Venice with him looking like a zombie. I fucking hated myself. Therefore, don't fuck your friends, especially if you want them in your life forever, and Anas was someone I wanted in my life forever. But I lost him. I lost that friendship for life, and I still miss his friendship every day."

"You can't take all the credit for every heart you've broken. People change. People grow. People's needs transform. Everyone plays a role in love. Love is about taking risks too. It's dangerous. But that's what's so exciting about it. If your friendship with Anas was as close as you say, he would have known the truth in your heart. He would have known when you left London, there was a chance you would change. Fuck, it sounds like you wanted to change. You wanted more. You were searching for something, weren't you? He would have known there was a chance you might find it. He would have known what you were looking for out there wasn't him when you left. He was just in denial. We all like to avoid the hard stuff. It sounds like Anas did a good job at that too. You got to stop beating yourself up and taking responsibility for everyone else's pain and just worry about your own, or you'll never get out alive. You need to forgive yourself, pick up the pieces, and just keep being you without fucking apologising for it. You won't get back what you lost, but you're not a bad person." Brian's words gave me shivers.

"You're right. Damn my wild heart!" I smiled as I looked into his eyes before getting out of the taxi.

"But that's what's so beautiful about it." He smiled back before he kissed me. I would not soon forget.

Chapter 10

It hadn't been a pleasant atmosphere on the boat for a few days. The wind picked up fast, reaching a high-speed twenty-five knots. It was so strong it ripped the number one headsail straight down the middle. The number one was the largest sail we had and was most useful when there was little wind, or we wanted more power to go faster. The weather became heavy, scary, looming waves reaching for the stern.

Andy came out to helm because the wind and swell became too much for me. Things always went wrong in rough conditions. The boys had spent all day trying to fix the alternator and rewire the generator. We needed both in working order for power. They had been trying to figure out why the batteries were losing power.

It took a few days, but the wind eventually dropped right off. It wasn't ideal as it meant we weren't moving any closer to Djibouti, and the crew was getting restless, bored, and irritated with each other.

I was frustrated I had run out of time in Suez to find an internet café to speak with Steve. I was trying to course-correct by not avoiding difficult conversations. This was important. I was angry at myself for not taking charge and making this step a priority; instead, I had become distracted getting stoned at the shisha café and lapping up all the attention from a bunch of local guys. *For fuck's sakes, Renee.*

Not only that, I was frustrated with the rest of the crew too. But on a much smaller scale. And in petty ways. Little things just started to get on my nerves. Which happens if you spend enough time with anyone, their idiosyncrasies start to grate on your bones. I wasn't the only one feeling it. The crew was getting frustrated with each other.

Nikki appeared to be getting a bit big for her boots, assigning herself to the role of the mother hen. She told me how much she resented cleaning up after the boys. I didn't know why she felt like she had to clean up after them. No one had asked her to. Her resentment appeared to be building by the hour as she bossed everyone around to clean up after themselves because she'd had enough. I loved her to bits, but I could see how the boys looked at her that sent a clear message she was annoying them. I especially don't take well to being told what to do. I could put up with Lee being demanding because of his position, but not a fellow crew member. One of the main reasons I loved to travel was I didn't have to answer to anyone. I did what I wanted to do when I wanted to do it.

Then there was Andy, who had become somewhat possessive over his lighters. I didn't understand why we couldn't just leave the fucking lighters in one place and share them. Maybe it was just me being selfish because I didn't have one. I needed one to cook with and smoke with. I was being a tight ass and needed to buy one in Djibouti. Then I'd tie it to my wrist, just to be a smartass.

The mother sun was burning with a bite in the vastness of the empty blue sky. I attempted to stay out of her way as much as possible. I couldn't understand how the crew could just sunbake and listen to the same music every day. Well, not every day, but when it was quiet, and the days seemed repetitive like groundhog day. I didn't understand why they didn't seem to care about skin cancer or turning into leathery old prunes. I wondered whether they had the same sun safety messages in their countries. I also didn't know why I was sounding like my mother. *Whatever.* It was just another stupid thing that irritated me about them.

I just needed some space. We all need space from each other. I'm sure I pissed them off too. The only person I wasn't sick of was Brian. The others were probably sick of our lovey-dovey shit.

We found some excitement in changing our clothes for the first time in three days. I loved the bohemian lifestyle and would have been fine, leaving behind the superficial. The material. All of what was unnecessary and didn't matter. Instead, I could bathe in all that did. Love. Growth. Peace. But on that day, all those things were not enough. We needed to wash in soapy water.

It also gave me a chance to gaze upon Brian's insanely fit body. He dragged a bucket beside the boat filling it with water. The sweat on his arms appeared glossy as he tensed to pull the bucket up and lifted it over his head. His muscles bulged with a definition. His eyes closed in anticipation as he emptied the bucket. A waterfall drenched his glistening body. I bit my bottom lip. It was red hot. I was sure I did not look as sexy as that when it came to my turn. I could barely manage to pull the water bucket back up, the rope clumsily slipping from my hands. My face wrinkled tense with strain. Brian giggled, watching me try until he came over to help me, lifting it easily high above my head and dunking me in the cold salt water. I looked more like a drowned rat coming out of a swamp than a professional athlete like him.

We washed the salt water off with fresh water from a hose that connected the water supply. I savoured the precious fresh feeling after washing, shaving, and brushing my teeth and hair because it never lasted long once the salt realised you were clean and needed to repossess you for the sea.

Brian and I started to think we were going nuts one night on our watch. We talked about absolute rubbish, singing nursery rhymes and reciting any poetry we could remember. I thought I saw a whale and Brian thought it was a dolphin until we realised it was just a wave.

I sat singing to myself for an hour, rocking back and forth. Then I cleaned the fridge. It wasn't working, but it was covered in mould. It felt like the smallest of chores took so much longer on the boat, or maybe I was just more mindful and took more time to do them because being time-efficient was not a factor. I needed things to do anyway.

To fill the time, I cooked every meal I could, even cleaned up after! I practised hoisting and pulling down sails every chance I could. I played cards with Nikki. I practised sailing manoeuvres like jibing. Jibing was dangerous as fuck because we had to turn with the wind as opposed to into the wind by swinging the sail from one side of the boat to the other. It was scary because when the sail wasn't full of wind, it would make a loud noise like shotguns going off all around you.

I found a sailing coursebook on board. Brian motivated me to work through it. I also learned the phonetic alphabet. The phonetic alphabet was important because if you needed to use the VHF radio to communicate with other boats or ports, you would have to use the phonetic alphabet to spell the name of your boat. I wanted to learn how to have the skills to use the VHF radio so that, touch wood, if I ever found myself in an emergency, I could radio out for help. It started to make me feel safe again. Learning these new skills gave me confidence in taking ownership over my own life as I began to feel more capable and comfortable with the responsibility of taking care of the lives of the crew. I was picking up the pieces and putting them back together.

The trip had been wonderful so far besides Lee's crap. His moodiness was putting a huge downer on the day-to-day, moment-to-moment experience. Lee had frequently been snapping criticisms at the crew. I was proud of what I had achieved and had gained some competencies in understanding sailing manoeuvres, techniques, and skills in the five weeks on board. But my gained experience still wasn't sufficient to keep me safe from Lee's harsh criticism.

"You've all been on this boat for a month; you should know what you're doing by now!"

It was contradictory to his initial response when we first met whether he would accept a crew member who had no previous sailing experience. Maybe he, too, had changed his mind on where he stood with that. Perhaps juggling the responsibilities of the boat's repairs, mapping courses, and teaching the crew to sail was proving too much for him. But, recently, I had noticed he seemed to single me out more than the rest of the crew. I thought it was just in my head, but I mentioned it to Brian, who also had noticed it. We couldn't think of a reason he would be upset with me more than anyone else.

It had come out of nowhere. It wasn't a progressive disliking towards me. It was like a switch had flipped, and Lee turned into an "asshole," as Fazi would put it. Brian told me not to worry about it. But it didn't stop the harsh criticisms cutting deep into the wounds I was already trying to lick. I felt broken down by his shit. I struggled to deal with how his behaviour left me feeling about myself. I sensed Lee's nonsense hurt me more than it would have before the rape, because I hadn't yet grown back my confidence to shield myself from toxic stuff. I feared talking to him about it and continued to allow him to speak to me that way. I felt the same fear of speaking up after the rape coming back to haunt me.

I knew Brian had to resist saying something either out of respect for Lee's position on the crew or the culture of not questioning the skipper's authority. It caused me sometimes to doubt whether I deserved to be on the boat. It made me feel like getting off at the next place we docked and flying home. It sounded so much easier just to quit. Considering leaving gave me back some sense of power. Just in knowing I could.

It would have been easy to scream, "*Fuck you, Lee. You're an asshole!*" And then give him the finger, turn my back, and head in the direction of the nearest airport. *But where's the satisfaction in that?*

If I left, I wouldn't have been around to watch him suffer from one less crew member for the rest of the trip to Phuket. I also would have let down the rest of the crew. And that was what I was used to doing. Letting people down and running away. That was my usual dance, and I was bored with the steps. It was the same painting I was tired of looking at on the wall, the lyrics I had grown weary of singing. I wanted to rewrite the song. That sounded like more fun than just continuing to do the same old shit I had been doing since the rape.

My revenge would be to finish what I had started. I promised myself I would try my best to push through it, to take every day as it comes. That would be my way of flipping Lee the bird. I reminded myself I could do hard things and learn to sit with my feelings. If I needed to talk, I had Brian and my journal. I would reclaim what Ryan stole from me on the dirty carpeted floor of the deserted room, at the bottom of the stairs, on that dark, terrible night. *Fuck you too, Ryan.*

Step 4. Sing Over Your Bones

"The world will see you the way you see you, and treat you the way you treat yourself."

BEYONCE

Chapter 11

I missed the smell of the rain as much as I missed home. Would it smell the same out at sea? Five weeks into the trip and we still hadn't seen rain. The sun had turned on us just as Lee's behaviour had taken a turn for the worse. The deck felt like hot sand under the soles of my feet. I hopscotched on the tips of my toes onto a towel to helm. The scorching sun put the crew's sunbaking goals on standby.

The galley was like an infrared sauna. I took pleasure in watching the sweat trickle down my body, visualising every droplet engorged with the stagnant, toxic shit I had stored inside my bones that was now being released. It was the same feeling I get listening to heavy metal music after the lead singer screams his lungs out. I'm left with a big smile because they just did the very thing my soul wants to do.

Brian, Nikki, and Andy didn't look like they were enjoying the detox process as much I was, their faces contorted with looks of desperation. Dehydration was a risk factor, so it was important to make sure we drank plenty of water.

"It's only going to get hotter!" Lee looked up with an amused joker grin.

When the sun was easing up on us late in the afternoon, the crew would venture up on deck for fresh air. Flocks of birds would come to rest on the boat. A few cheeky birds landed on the crew's heads. Lee told us the birds settled on the vessel because they were suffering from the heat, too; some would eventually die from exhaustion.

I turned my head and whispered to the bird that had landed on my shoulder, "Rest your wings, songbird. You will fly again soon. Home is waiting for you."

The birds quickly added to Lee's stress as he became fearful they might break the wind instruments on top of the mast, which was the tallest part of the boat that held up the sail and balanced the boat. We needed all its parts in good working condition.

We continued to experience more mechanical failures. The steering failed in the middle of busy shipping lanes. Shipping lanes were like highways for ships, and they were just as dangerous to cross. Not long after that issue was fixed, the engine failed. Except for this time, it was much more serious because we drifted close to shore, which put us in danger of running aground. We could see the Yemen coastline on one side and Ethiopia's coastline on the other. Both were rocky coastlines and notorious for pirates. We put up the sails and gave it our best effort to tack out of the straits in the blistering heat.

The hardest part was tacking our way through crowded shipping lanes. Tacking involved manoeuvring the boat in a series of angles to stay on the same course. And we did this in the dark to exit the bottleneck of the Red Sea. All the ships we had passed through the Suez Canal were suddenly caught in gridlock traffic trying to enter the Indian Ocean. We had to be super focused, communicate clearly, and stay on our game. It was strenuous on our bodies as it stretched the crew's experience. Each member gritted their teeth as they reached deep for any energy left within our dehydrated bodies to give everything; we had to work together to get us to safety. This marathon effort took us forty-eight hours to accomplish.

I loved the opportunity to put to practice all the technical skills I had learned about sailing. It was thrilling, even though it was super hard and had the potential to be very dangerous. Brian and I enjoyed the chance to find our rhythm and dance, moving with each other to pull off some tricky manoeuvres. I thoroughly enjoyed this and felt much more confident and a valuable member of the team. This was the moment I felt I shined as a crew member. I was realising I could do dangerous things and not only survive but also have awesome fun at the same time!

I noticed I was improving by the day. It was about growing confidence. I had what it took to look after myself. I was starting to trust other people to take care of me too. I felt I was reaping the benefits of leaving my comfort zone. I was trying new things and stepping out of my own way. These risks were about growth. They weren't coming from a place of fear anymore. I let go of the self-harm and the avoidance that only resulted in me disrespecting my body.

This was the freedom I had been searching for in my travels. My head was now listening to my heart and what it needed to feel strong again. Stronger than I had ever been before. I was living my truth. I was learning to lean into everything hard. I was learning not to run away. Not to avoid. I was a match for my mountain—the *obstacle* was the way home. I had discovered the map to get there, and I was strong enough to make the journey.

But with every gain, there came another challenge around the corner, looking for a way to test the lessons I was learning. To shake the strength of the new foundations that were being set.

Lee spotted a boat motoring at high speed, heading straight towards us. He woke Brian alarmed.

"Nikki and Renee, I'm giving you your passports. If anything happens to us, you know how to sail the boat now. I have written the coordinates down for where you can find help. You sail in that direction and stay off the radio. Now hide, please."

There was no time to ask questions. We could only guess it

wasn't good. *What is happening?*

It all happened so fast. Lee handed us our passports, and then we rushed down the companionway to our room. We stood in our cabin with the door closed, somewhat frozen for a moment as we tried to figure out what to do and where to hide. I grabbed a high heel from my cupboard. It was the only thing I could find to use as a weapon.

I suggested to Nikki we should hide in the forward locker. Quietly and as smoothly as possible, we made our way in and hid under various items and a wool blanket. It was sweltering with heat. The sweat trails felt like snakes slithering silently and constricting my airways, their tongues occasionally flicking out to taste the fear in the air.

"What's the worst that can happen, Renee?" Nikki asked with a quiver in her voice.

"The boys get murdered. We're left on the boat to find help. We get trafficked and gang-raped," I answered with unusual certainty.

"Isn't death worse?" Nikki responded.

"Not for me," I answered.

"Yeah, you're probably right." Nikki looked up at a small window to see if she could see anything.

I reached out to Nikki, guiding her back to hide under the covers.

I looked straight into Nikki's eyes, full of fear staring back at me, and said, "Whatever happens, I'm going to survive."

"*Me too.*" Nikki smiled back. And just like that, we had our survival plan.

A sudden boom shook the entire boat and rattled every bone in my body. Another boat had connected with ours. Then a fast, foreign language. Harsh voices of men with aggressive tones. I closed my eyes and prayed for the crew's safety, silently holding onto Nikki's hand as tightly as I could. I tried not to shake and to remain as still as possible in case they searched the boat. It felt like we were hiding in the front head on the verge of tears for a lifetime.

Brian came down to tell us the coast was clear by yelling, "GET UP!" in a deep, scary voice.

We both jumped in fright. Brian took off fast through our cabin and up the companionway onto the deck. I ran straight after him, grabbing at his singlet. I caught up to him and landed a solid punch in the arm.

"Are you fucking serious? You think that's funny, Brian? You're an asshole!" I yelled at him with tears in my eyes.

He had no idea what I had already been through and what thoughts had been going through my mind. I also wasn't ready to tell him the whole backstory behind my fear. However, I explained just how shit scared Nikki and I had been in that moment, and for him to make a joke like that was fucking downright cruel.

"I'm sorry! Come here." Brian pulled me in close and wrapped me in his arms.

I buried my face in his chest to hide my tears—his hand stroking my hair.

"I didn't know you were that scared. I'm sorry. I feel amazing. You should have seen me." Brian appeared to be on a high and excited by his experience.

Fearless motherfucker. I wiped my face and sat down to listen as he continued.

"They said they were Eritrean Navy, but they didn't have any uniforms on. They were dressed in basketball shirts and holding machine guns. They wanted us to give them DVDs and DVD players. But we told them we were a poor boat with no DVDs.

They wanted to see our passports. But I insisted on seeing their passports. They weren't official Navy, that's for sure. I tried to hustle them for diesel instead. It was awesome. I wished you could have seen it. We talked them out of their own game!"

He spoke loudly, as if he was telling an old war story at the pub. I tried to be happy for him, but I couldn't feel anything. I smiled back at him, pretending to give him the attention and praise he was looking for, but I was in shock.

"Sorry to do that to you girls," Lee added. "I didn't want to complicate matters by introducing Western women into the equation. Human trafficking and the hostage and ransom business in these areas is a thriving economy. I had to take the situation very seriously."

Nikki and I shared a glance that spoke volumes. We had no idea of the risks that were involved when we accepted this trip. We were still very shaken but laughed about it a few hours later after sunset. No one was hungry until late that night.

We slept five nights, anchored off Djibouti.

"Land of the unlucky," as Lee put it.

The people who live in Djibouti were Somalian, Ethiopian, and Yemen refugees.

"But if they survived the wars in their countries, maybe they're the lucky ones," I suggested, which Lee ignored.

It made me wonder what barriers these displaced people had to endure and overcome to create new homes for themselves in Djibouti. Did they face negative attitudes from the citizens? Did some citizens say things to them like, "You should go back to where you came from," just as they did in Australia? Did their countries of birth cancel their citizenship for fleeing for safety? Could they still practice their culture and speak their language free from fear of violence? Were they able to find a community they could belong to? Were they able to reconnect with their family? Did they feel safe?

I related to the sense of being forced out of one's home, whether that home was a physical place or an emotional place, resulting in running and searching for a place of protection. I didn't know war, only the war I was fighting in my head, but I was drawn to stories of genocide since the rape. I became a dark tourist in an attempt to understand how human beings can commit evil acts.

A documentary on the weaponisation of rape in Central Africa for war and profit continued to come to mind. I learned that in most traditional cultures, rape broke down the family system. The status quo believed that women who had experienced rape were dirty and disgraced the entire family. The cultures relied heavily on the reputation of their name for trade and marriage prospects, which left them thinking they had no choice but to banish any woman who threatened that.

After an entire village was attacked, targeting women to rape, the village cast out the women who were assaulted. It left them vulnerable, rejected, grieving the loss of their families, and the only way of life they had ever known, with no prospects. The women left wounded couldn't physically run in search of safety. The sacred place between their legs left broken and bleeding—the sacred place that gave life; life to babies, babies that would eventually grow into men, men just like the rapists themselves. The women were left helpless, to crawl and drag their soiled bodies through the mountainous jungles to the closest city, a journey that could take weeks.

And if they were lucky not to bleed out, be attacked by a wild animal, or snatched up again by the militia to continue abusing, then they might find safety, in which case, they would need to start the slow recovery process. These women might never have children again, and more often than not, they require vaginal reconstruction surgery to allow their bladder and bowel to function.

What was left of their village quickly fell apart. The village men found themselves unable to farm the long hours, look after the household responsibilities, and care for the children. Whole villages had to make the heartbreaking decision to leave their land. This was the land that generations of their family had farmed and raised families on. Now they had to move to the city. They simply could not survive if they stayed. Entire villages had fallen victim to their cultural attitudes towards rape, playing straight into the palms of evil that orchestrated the mobilisation of local militia forces for mining companies to profit.

I could never comprehend the gravity of what these survivors had suffered and the mountains they had climbed to create a new place to call "home," but I could try to *learn*.

I could *listen*. I could sit with their stories and *not turn away* when their tales became too much for my heart to bear.

As an Australian citizen, I would most likely never have to experience anything like the suffering of these women in Central Africa. The only thing that separated our experiences was the countries we were born in and the colour of my skin. I had the privilege of being able to return to the country and land I grew up on.

The pain I felt from witnessing the lack of opportunity in Djibouti and the privilege I had struck me. I felt depressed. Something had woken inside me, and I couldn't go back to sleep. I felt this stirring that I was on the verge of discovering something big that would help me sing. I felt this calling to service. To take action to help people who were suffering. It felt strong, whatever it was. And I couldn't ever go back to sleep again. Not with this knowing. Not ever. I had to do something. I couldn't sit on the sidelines and be a bystander. I wouldn't. I refused. No chance. Not now. I knew what I had to do. My course had been set, and it wasn't a man I was sailing home for anymore. I found something better. I found direction. I started to realise that my existence in this world was important, and the world needed me. I was born to do *great* things, not just hard things. My sensitivity led me here. My empathy gave me this gift. My bones felt like they were coming back to life as they surged with purpose and shook with excitement.

Chapter 12

Nikki and I dug deep to find the courage to approach Lee about how his moods had been affecting us. We chose the perfect moment after he had a few beers under his belt.

"Don't take it to heart, girls. It's nothing personal."

I felt relieved. But I sensed there was more to be revealed than what his light-hearted, casual, and somewhat dismissive response suggested.

I had spotted an Australian flag flying in the breeze on a nearby sailing boat that reminded me I had bigger things to deal with. I had to get to an internet café ASAP to speak with Steve. Every day that I didn't talk to him since deciding to let him go felt like a betrayal, not only to Steve but also to my own truth. He needed to know that there were more layers to coming home than I was aware of at the start of the trip.

On my mission to finally connect with Steve, Andy and I were escorted by a Yemen man who picked us up by boat taxi and dropped us at the port. He introduced us to a guide who accompanied us in a taxi into town and guided us to where we needed to go, all for a small discretionary payment for his service.

I could not find any internet cafes where I could make an international phone call. I decided I would have to settle for email. It wasn't ideal, but I wasn't left with any choice.

I was halfway through typing the longest email I had ever typed in my life when the café had a blackout. *WTF!*

I lost the email and had to start all over again. It took me two hours to rewrite it and click send. It was out there now and on its way to Steve to read. I knew he wouldn't respond like Anas; by completely cutting me out of his life. However, I still worried it was a possibility. I hoped Steve would understand.

Brian was happy to hear I had stepped up and did the right thing by emailing Steve. To celebrate, we had kebabs for dinner, even though I'd heard the food in Africa could make you sick if you weren't used to it. Brian and I headed back to the boat around ten-pm.

Lee appeared to be upset with us. He didn't speak or make any eye contact. We assumed he must have been angry because we had spent time off the boat whilst he was sleeping from a hangover all day. Before we arrived in Djibouti, Lee briefed us on his expectations: day one, we would arrive at the port and get drunk. Day two, sleep, rest, and start boat work. Day three, finish off boat work. Day four, free day to sight-see.

Lee seemed to send mixed messages by disappearing and returning late at night. If he could enjoy his day off the boat, then why couldn't we? *Is he jealous? Is he scared we wouldn't come back?* I didn't understand why he was so controlling but then being inconsistent about it too.

It was the uncertainty that fucked with my head. *Would he prefer for us to just sit around all day and wait for him to wake up to find out what he would like us to do?* I fucking hated being superglued to the crew, and this ridiculous idea we had to bow down to keep the skipper "fat and happy." It was a load of shit. I wasn't interested in subservience, and I began to resent Lee.

Provisioning the boat with diesel and water had been a pain in the ass in Djibouti. Food provisioning had been extremely expensive, but supermarkets were easy to come by. Because of the expense, we were forced to keep portions small and meals simple. Brian taught Nikki and me how to drive the dingy to help deliver water to the boat. I loved adding another new skill to my tool belt.

Nikki and I buckled down and completed all our boat tasks in one day. We packed away neatly all the gear that had been pulled out to dry from the forward locker, folded up the sails and tied them to the deck, cleaned the esky, deck, cooker, forward head, and galley. We only stopped for lunch and finished just as the sun began to set at seven pm.

I relished in some much-needed girl time alone with Nikki. We didn't get to spend much time together at all. We were on separate watches, which meant when I was awake, she was asleep, and vice versa. When we were awake, it was usually when we were busy in the common spaces doing things like cooking, reading, or journaling. Nikki must have felt very isolated since Brian and I had gotten close.

It didn't feel safe to approach Nikki in front of Lee to say, "Hey, can we have some girl time and catch up in private?"

I was worried it would have come off secretive, and I didn't want any additional unwanted attention from Lee, so I was cautious about what I said in front of him. But this time, we were alone, and we didn't have to censor ourselves; I felt comfortable and able to speak freely to her about my experience so far, and it seemed like she did too. I felt energised just being able to share some time and space to laugh loudly together about the funny idiosyncrasies of the crew, the constant mechanical failures, Lee's moods, the personal adjustments to life at sea, my relationship with Brian, the fact we were in Africa on a sailing boat, etc. We laughed about it all.

It felt like we were two little girls just being ourselves, having a tea party outside in the sun. Not a worry in the world. We finished the day, and I gave Nikki a high-five and a tender hug that lasted enough time for her to know she meant a lot to me, and she wasn't alone. I appreciated our combined effort getting the boat in order and the simple joy the day had brought to both of us, especially getting to see her big, bright smile that could revive the dead. She was special.

~

We had heard of a Russian boat robbed of valuables during the night whilst the crew slept.

"It's a business here. The locals at port ask if you require security. If you say no, they rob you. They're all in on it. Even the marina police," Lee informed us.

Lee thought we would be protected by paying a local to stay on deck for the duration of our stay. This made perfect sense, but not the part about paying someone to do a job and then not trusting him to do it. Lee was not willing to take any chances, so he made one of the crew stay behind at all times.

He decided that Brian and I would stay behind and watch the boat whilst he, Nikki, and Andy went into town for dinner and drinks. Lee told us that when Andy returned, we could head out. I was in a heavy strop again about not being able to leave the boat. I felt we earned the right to enjoy ourselves after Nikki, and I gave so much love to the boat all day. It felt like a kick in the guts.

I acted like I did as a teenager when I was grounded for doing the wrong thing and told I wasn't allowed to go to a friend's party. I sulked as I laid down on my side on the deck, my arm dangling into the water while thinking, *Fuck you, Lee*, as I watched Brian drive the dinghy to drop the crew at the port.

On his way back, Brian changed directions. He motored towards the boat with the Australian flag that I had noticed earlier. An elderly couple came out to greet him as he reached up to shake their hands. I didn't know what he was doing but I felt jealous. *Why is he going to talk to the Australian people on the boat?*

It wasn't until he came back that I understood he did it for me. I missed home so much.

"I told them I had a homesick Australian girlfriend on board. I asked them if they wouldn't mind helping to cheer up a sad Australian girl who missed home."

His thoughtfulness and the fact he knew being around my people would make me smile made my heart swell.

"What the fuck! You are fucking incredible. Do you know that? And you just called me your girlfriend." I kissed him, scrambling to find my footing on the dinghy.

"I did too." He laughed.

I could have dived into the water and swam over. I was that excited to meet them. Brian drove me over to the Australians' boat and introduced me. I was starting to miss home immensely.

"G'day, *mate!*"

The lovely couple from Brisbane chose an Australian greeting instead of using hello. I was overjoyed just listening to them speak; their accents familiar. They immediately invited us onto their beautiful yacht and made me feel like I was at home again.

They had decided not to have children and instead spent their lives heavily consumed by their careers. Upon retirement, they knew they wanted more from life than the mundane, so they sold everything, bought a yacht, and wanted to spend the rest of their time sailing around the world.

We exchanged travel stories over a few red wines and an anti-pesto platter. This was Australian hospitality at its best.

Their sailing boat was very comfortable, to say the least, unlike our boat that was falling apart by the day. Theirs was fully enclosed, sheltered from the elements with air conditioning and expensive, plush carpet that felt like heaven under my feet. They told us their boat is super easy to sail. They simply type in their coordinates, and the boat auto-helms. They have never had an issue with their engine or auto-helm. They even had a computer that would hoist the right sails for them, depending on the weather conditions. *Wow.* It was hard not to wonder whether they were really sailing. They certainly weren't suffering like we were.

It was a struggle not to compare boats, just like it's hard not to compare stories sometimes. We can never truly know someone else's experiences. Even if their vessel might appear more expensive or a little prettier, it doesn't mean their boat offers an experience that is of any less or more value. Just like we are, as people, no less or more value than each other, we are all equally worthy and deserving of love.

Brian and I returned to the boat just before Lee and Nikki flashed a torchlight from port to signal us to pick them up in the dinghy.

Leaving the Australian couple was hard and deep down, I wanted to ask if they could take me home. I could have cried in their arms and begged them to take me with them. Instead, I went back to my own *imperfect* boat with Brian.

Chapter 13

Lee looked furious and asked to have a chat with me. I began to panic. *Fuck.*

It was clear someone had a 'bitch session' for him to want to talk almost immediately after returning from town. He looked infuriated. I looked at Brian nervously. He gave me a look that I read as saying, "Good luck!"

"I want to talk to you about some issues that have raised concern. You delayed the trip a week by not being available until after La Tomatina Festival. You then lost people's money by delaying it further by getting ill. We had to stop in Sardinia for your treatment. This was your fault because you did not prepare yourself with adequate medical supplies. And you need to replace the two packets of pain killers you finished."

This was crazy. I had asked whether it was okay for us to leave when I got back from the festival, and Lee agreed to it. Now he was throwing it back in my face. *And how the fuck is it my fault I got a gum infection? How is it my fault people lost money because I needed medical attention? Isn't it the responsibility of the owner to take care of the crew? Does he want me to pay the money back?*

I had no idea I was going to get a gum infection. I'd never had one before. I didn't buy any painkillers because I avoided using them most of the time. I had never sailed before, so how could I possibly foresee needing to provision myself with medical supplies? Painkillers cost a couple of bucks—it wasn't even that big of a deal. I was livid with rage.

"And what's your opinion about provisioning?"

"I worried about it, to begin with, but I'm over it now. We will make do. We're all in the same boat, literally," I replied, attempting to be as agreeable as could be.

"You also treat Brian like the skipper and not me."

"I'm sorry; that's not my intention. I guess I do all of my watches with Brian, so I'm used to answering to him."

"You have been sneaking around, hiding chocolates and cokes."

"I haven't hidden anything. Brian sends me down to collect cokes and chocolates for him whilst we're on watch."

"You've been making teams and alliances. You are just isolating yourself from the crew, and you need to grow up!"

I knew without a doubt that someone had had a good bitch about me. *Where is this bullshit coming from? Had he stored all this up in his mind?*

This explained why he had been acting like such an asshole for the last few weeks. He had created a long list of reasons he resented me.

"I want us to leave Djibouti as one team. We still have a month until we reach Thailand, and we need each other to make it work. I'm happy with your progress and input. Nothing will matter once we reach Thailand. You'll be so proud of yourself, and I know you will get so much out of this experience."

I agreed.

"I miss home, and I've been feeling unhappy because I want more time on land rather than being on the boat when we're in port. Originally, we spoke about enjoying the places we stopped at on the way to Thailand. But it doesn't seem like we have the freedom to do much. I'm grateful for the opportunity to do this and for you taking a chance on me having no experience. And I'm sorry for anything I've done to give you a poor opinion of me and for slowing the boat's progress down."

"It's nothing personal, and at the end of the day, it's just business," he finished.

I hugged him. I played my hand with kindness, and I hated myself for it. It reminded me of something the nasty girls at school would do when pretending to be my friend. This was not me at all. It was not who I was raised to be.

I was raised to always be honest. When I was thirteen, I was caught smoking in the school toilets by my music teacher. I was disciplined with three days of detention, and they made me write a letter home to inform my parents of the rule I had broken.

In my family, honesty was everything. If you lied, you were dead! I knew I had to fess up before that letter arrived home. I sat at the dinner table that night, nervously twitching in my seat, my palms sweating as I tried to build up the nerve to tell them the truth and face their impending disappointment. I took a big breath and exhaled, then I told them I had been caught smoking in the toilets.

Mum and dad smiled at each other from opposite ends of the table.

Mum asked, "Are you going to do it again?"

"No!" I blurted out close to tears.

"Okay. Thanks for being honest."

That was it. No punishment because they valued honesty over everything else. However, outside of my family home, the world taught me something very different.

During my school years, I found that most girls just pretended to be my friend because, deep down, they were jealous. I was a natural leader, confident speaking up to help anyone in need. I wasn't afraid to throw a punch, swear, or challenge a bully. I spoke up about students' rights. I even wrote a letter to the local newspaper about how teacher strikes were impacting our education. I challenged some teachers on grading by comparing their marks across students' papers to ensure they were consistent. Let's face it; I was a bit of a pain in the ass. But I wouldn't just remain silent and let shit happen around me if I knew it was wrong.

This made my female peers uncomfortable with me as they compared themselves. They wanted to have the confidence to speak up. I know this because, after school, some of them told me usually after one too many drinks at a party. They too, wanted to tell the boys to fuck off when they were jerks. They too, wanted to tell the girls to stop being bitches to each other. They too, wanted to stand up to the teachers for the grades they had worked their asses off. But because I did it, some girls turned nasty.

Someone even slandered my name by writing "Renee Simpson's a SLUT" in thick black marker pen so many times on the walls of the school bathroom that there was no space for me to write a reply. The school had to repaint the entire toilet block. There were over 600 girls that attended the school and one large toilet block. Every girl at school knew my name after that. By this time, I was fourteen years old, and the world had taught me it didn't value honesty.

I learnt that I would pay the price for refusing to become another sheep. I rejected the idea of watering myself down to make others feel more comfortable with themselves. I preferred the lonelier path if it meant compromising on who I was. The world just didn't feel like a safe place for me to be honest anymore.

My honesty with Anas cost me his friendship. My honesty in speaking to Michelle about the rape had cost me friendships. I was afraid of how my honesty was about to impact Steve. And this is why I faked it with Lee because I feared he wouldn't be able to handle my honesty and punish me for it.

I had felt strange all day with bad cramps in my stomach. I

wondered if my body was responding to me, bottling up my honesty. Brian and I went out to a bar for beers, but I couldn't even finish one. I wanted to drink and have a good night out, but I just couldn't stomach it. Andy was in bed all day and night, ill with food poisoning. I knew we were about to get hit next. Sure enough, the next day, I felt terrible. Stomach cramps and nausea galore. *Welcome, food poisoning. I've been waiting for you.*

"Brian, what if I need to do a number two?"

"I would suggest avoiding the toilet at all costs until it passes."

I took his wise advice. I didn't move from the comfort of my bed all day. I felt so guilty about not being able to contribute anything to work on the boat. I worried about getting sick for an extended period again, especially after Lee's harsh criticism. I was sure Lee thought I was faking it just to get out of work.

Nikki, Lee, and Brian went to have a few beers while I went back to bed to rest. Saying no to beer was the real indicator that I wasn't well.

"Too sick to drink! Fuck, you must be dying, Renee. Someone take her to a hospital!" That's what my dad would say.

I recovered and bounced back to full health overnight. We left when everyone was awake. Brian and I were the first ones up, keen to get a move on. We set sail for Sri Lanka.

Halfway through the day, Brian was in bed with stomach cramps and nausea. He lived off kebabs in Djibouti and was now vomiting and had diarrhoea for a day and a half. Just a few days prior, I warned him about taking it easy with the local food.

Brian laughed it off with, "No, I'll be fine. I have an iron stomach." I had to remind him about his remark.

"Well, Mr Iron Stomach. Who's laughing now?"

He laughed as he still managed to pull himself out of bed

whilst feeling like death to help Lee with mechanical problems. He even got up to help me on our watch. He was a trooper.

He recovered after two days. I prayed this leg of the trip would be kind to us, and the hard parts were behind us.

Chapter 14

"You're not sailing if you're not sore!" Brian yelled out from the helm over the wind.

I had to toughen up quickly. We came up against strong winds and currents. These heavy weather conditions were the most challenging we had come across so far. Remaining on course was impossible, and we were slowed down, adding extra days to our ETA.

Helming became tough on my arms. My back ached, and we were making several tacks a watch in crazy heavy weather. I had grazes, cuts, and bruises all over my legs and my nails kept breaking. The saltwater stung the unhealed cuts. We changed into wet weather gear at night, even though it wasn't wet, just cold. The crew was tremendously worn out. If we were not on watch, we were sleeping.

After a few days, my body adjusted to the physical demand. I was staying awake for twelve hours. I strived to keep myself busy by doing chores or journaling. We filled the esky with water from Djibouti to wash our clothes.

The system was to wash clothes in a bucket of saltwater with washing powder and then rinse them out in the esky of Djibouti water. We pegged our clothes to anything we could to dry in the wind. It took three days for our clothes to dry because the waves kept splashing them. Even after being washed, my clothes smelled like a street dog.

My khaki shorts had completely ripped and fallen apart to the point I couldn't wear them anymore, and my black shorts had holes in the ass of them. This meant I only had one pair of shorts left. The saltwater was just rotting our clothes away. If this had continued, I would have soon been known as the nude sailor from Australia.

I needed a new wardrobe. I had been wearing the same backpack of clothes for eighteen months, only adding a pair of shorts and a couple of shirts here and there. That's what you do when you live the life of a frugal backpacker. It's all about saving as much money as you can for beers and parties! You eat one main meal a day and live off sandwiches and water. Well, that's what I did anyway.

Lee removed himself from watches because of the many repairs that needed his attention. His mood was lighter without the added pressure of watches, which made a massive difference to the atmosphere on the boat. He was in charge of cooking dinner because food provisions were low, and he wanted to make sure they lasted the distance. We were only allowed cereal for breakfast and the main meal for dinner. I knew provisioning was going to be an issue, but I remained silent in Djibouti. I feared we would have no choice but to stop for provisions before Sri Lanka.

One day, Nikki and I had an opportunity to demonstrate our sailing skills by hoisting the headsail on our own. The boys clapped and whistled. The fact that we could physically lift the headsail on our own was an act of willpower, determination, and ambition. It wasn't just a sail we were raising. It felt like we had lifted a flag, calling for all women to RISE UP, to take their place in the world. It was the result of every minute of practice, training, and hard work.

Nikki and I had reached a milestone, one we hadn't realised we even set for ourselves. Once we looked into each other's eyes, we knew we had reached it. We shared the moment. We had become, "Sisters doin' it for themselves." Thank you for the music, Eurythmics, and Aretha Franklin. The icing on the cake was the crew's standing ovation and applause. They recognised the strength had come from hours of practice because they knew the power needed to hoist that sail up on our own. Nikki and I held hands and took our bow. Mother Nature was a witness, and she was proud as punch of her girls. I felt ready for the next level. I wanted to go big. *Bring it on, Mumma!*

A few days later, I hoisted the sail entirely on my own. Not even with the support of a winch. I had placed a lot of value on being strong, honest, and independent, but this was different. My body was transforming and allowing me to achieve more than it ever could before. I was taking on the appearance of an Olympic swimmer. I was witnessing my strength and power increase by the day. I was feeling more significant than the girl who first walked onto the boat. I was feeling like she was walking taller. There was more to her now. She was taking up space in the world. Her feet were buried firmly into the earth that lay beneath the ocean bed.

I was beginning to grow the same thing I had seen in Sean. The same thing I now saw in Brian. I felt that love Anas was not afraid to feel. For the first time since the rape, I could look myself in the mirror and not feel ashamed. I liked the girl standing in front of me as she smiled back at me with pride. I was learning to sing the high notes!

Brian was an excellent teacher and was always more than happy to answer my questions. He explained the reasons behind each sailing manoeuvre. I knew how to set them up, but not why we did them. He taught me about currents, wind direction, and its effect on course. Brian was very patient with me. He made me feel safe, valued, and respected. Brian made me feel the opposite of how Ryan made me feel after his choice to rape me.

My favourite watch was the two to six-am because everyone

would be sleeping. It was just God and me. Brian would try to catch up on some sleep if the weather was fine. There was something magical about seeing the sunrise, the wind in my hair, the clouds in the sky, those first initial rays of light that stretched out perfectly like a mother's arms beckoning an embrace from her child. I was in love watching the colours change moment by moment. It looked like I was sailing in heaven.

There I was, this twenty-two-year-old girl sailing this fifty-three-foot boat named *Who Dares Wins* all on my own through the mirrored water of the Indian Ocean. Four people's lives in my hands, and they were all nestled in their sleeping bags below deck sound asleep, trusting me to look after them. And I knew how. I felt unstoppable. It was Mother Nature and me taking time to converse in the waters of her womb as they lapped against the bow. I could feel the life force returning as I breathed in the moment's beauty. I made promises with my soul to stain this memory on my bones forever, for lifetimes to come. A holiday destination I could always visit when times get tough. I could breathe properly for the first time since the rape.

The rape had thrown me off my boat, but I had clung onto that rope that trailed behind it with one hand. I had managed to swim with the vessel the whole time. This journey slowed the boat down and allowed me to catch up to it. To climb the ladder, return to the helm and take back control. I was finding the sense of freedom that I was truly seeking within.

On the thirty-ninth day, we caught a mahi-mahi fish the size of a small child. It was an intense fluorescent yellow colour with bright blue spots. I saw myself as a little girl lying on the deck, gasping for air with a hook in her mouth. I knew the fish was dying because its vibrant colours began to fade, and suddenly, with her final breath, she turned from a dazzling blue to white. Her blue spots remained like scars as she gasped her last breath.

Andy, unfazed by the moving changes in colour, victoriously stabbed a knife through its head with such ferocity that he punctured the esky lid. And in a matter of minutes, I witnessed the destructive force of man and how he can act with no conscience as he destroys beauty in the world.

I wept to myself.

Ryan had stolen the self-worth, confidence, and trust I had built in myself. I became indecisive, uncertain, afraid, and insecure because I couldn't keep myself safe that night. I couldn't read that Ryan had the potential to do evil things. I blamed myself for what had happened. I wept as that beautiful fish gave the fight of its life because I finally realised that the evil in the world was not my fault. I was not to blame for the rape or any of the abuse I had suffered. It had nothing to do with me. I wasn't a victim. I was a survivor, and I was setting myself free from the hook in my mouth.

I am still fighting. I am still breathing. And I am still alive.

Step 5. Breathe Life Into Yourself

"Suffering of the body is nothing compared to the suffering of the mind."

BUDDHA

Chapter 15

Seven days after leaving Djibouti, the atmosphere on the boat had become quite tense as boredom and worry about low provisions set in hard. I was feeling exhausted. My body didn't feel strained, but the inconsistent sleeping patterns, change in eating habits, the onset of cold weather, and the stress from a certain someone's moodiness was taking a toll on me.

It seemed like Brian was always helping Lee on our watches lately, either on some problem with the boat or just a general chit chat. While Brian was off with Lee, I was left to helm for most of the watch. I was frustrated at myself for feeling frustrated. I felt I had no right to such feelings, considering how much Brian had supported me. I told myself I should just be grateful and let it go. I made excuses that I was bored and looking for someone to blame for my restlessness. I tried to drown out my negativity by borrowing Brian's iPod and tuning out to the music. I wanted to transport myself somewhere else for a while.

Lee had gone three days without talking to me directly. He could be so opinionated. Everything he said he believed to be a fact, and he was not open or interested in anyone else's ideas. As soon as he opened his mouth, I zoned out. People who think they already know everything will never learn a thing. It's by listening and being open to new ideas that we learn more and allow ourselves to grow. I discovered because Lee ignored the ideas of others; I was closed off to anything he had to say, preferring to save my energy for balanced discussions with Brian. At least our conversations allowed us to learn from each other's perspective.

I gave Lee something to whine about because I had started to isolate myself for real this time. It was obvious even to me. I found myself locking the door to my room one day for some private time. It was only fifteen minutes before I was interrupted, and the door was pushed open.

Nikki had been freaking out because there was only one roll of toilet paper left per person. I shared one with Brian. I didn't give a shit. *Pardon the pun.* I would be just fine using a bucket of water and a hand towel if we ran out. There were more pressing things to be concerned about, like the fact we were down to two bottles of water each. My concern remained that we weren't dividing them out. I desperately wanted to trust the others, but when it's about survival, *can you really trust anyone?* Food was scarcely low, and I could not bear to bring myself to look in the cupboards.

Lee cooked dinner that night. Andy and I were the only ones who hadn't eaten, and I ate before Andy. After I dished up, I saw Lee lift the rice cooker lid as if to check that I had left enough for Andy. We all knew rations were tight, but Lee still insisted on making us feel uncomfortable at mealtime. The way he behaved made me feel guilty for eating. I was waking up pissed off because I was letting him get to me.

The day prior, I had tiptoed around him because I knew he was stressed about the engine not working again. It took me ten minutes to think about how I was going to phrase a question, searching for the right words to sound as nice, polite, and non-offensive as possible.

"Lee, how would you like me to prepare this fish?"

He looked at me with disgust and rolled his eyes, and said, "I don't care. Just don't use the oven. You do know we don't have much gas. You do know that, right?"

Like I was some fucking idiot. "Yes," I said meekly.

It was crazy that I would feel like I was towering over my doubts, and then in that same moment, this small insignificant man had the power to take it all away. What a head fuck and a half.

Another reason I had withdrawn from the crew was the confrontation with Lee in Djibouti. Trying to figure out who had betrayed me played on my mind. I didn't trust Nikki or Andy, and I even began to question whether I could trust Brian. It didn't sit right with me.

The crew knew Lee hated me. It was evident in the way they looked at me. Like I had become some fucking scapegoat. And a victim was the last thing I ever wanted to be seen as. Nikki and Andy had to survive their watches with Lee, so I'm sure they would have felt the need to side with him just to make their time bearable.

My dad used to play this mind control game with my brother and me where we had to side with him, or he would be an "asshole." It made me realise I had survived his bullshit, so I could get through this too.

Lee was a master manipulator. He would lift the crew up with positive feedback, but it didn't matter how hard I tried, he would put me down. I had regressed into the wounded child. The more he hurt me, the more I desperately wanted his approval. I was confused by my feelings. I had all I needed within myself and in Brian's beautiful support, yet I was still allowing myself to be tripped up by this other person who didn't treat me with respect.

Something told me Lee probably wouldn't have been so nasty if Brian and I were not together. Lee was just another nasty girl from school, but I couldn't get on the bus and go home like in my teenage years. I was stuck in a small space with the "asshole." I had to grit my teeth and bear it. I reminded myself I could do hard things.

I watched how Brian interacted with Lee and followed his lead. He had this way of speaking to people; saying nothing that could be used against him. It didn't work for me. Instead, I kept my mouth shut. I started to become reluctant to talk to Brian. I felt myself completely withdraw. I trusted him but not enough to share my insecurities with him anymore.

"Hey, where have you gone recently?" Brian asked, attempting to sing me back to him.

I looked up from fiddling with some lolly wrappers, attempting to make a fishing lure with some thread I bought in Djibouti to make friendship bracelets. "Just working through some stuff in my head. It's not you. You're wonderful."

"Don't shut me out. I'm right here with you. I'm on your team, you know. I know Lee has been horrible to you lately. I can see it's getting to you. It must be tough."

"It is. I hate making these fucking fishing lures, too," I said as tears welled up in my eyes.

I unsuccessfully tried to push them down as fast they came to the surface. Brian rubbed my back with one hand, still on the helm.

"It's going to be okay. Hey, look, dolphins!" Brian distracted me from my depression by pointing out the biggest pod of dolphins yet to be sighted.

We estimated there were about three hundred, splashing and feeding in unison. They were surfing the bow wave right up to the horizon.

"Lee's going to set up an episode of *The Simpson's* for the crew to watch on the TV tonight, and he's going to helm. I think he knows everyone's feeling pretty beaten down."

"Yeah, maybe he should realise that it's fucking him causing it."

Brian giggled, continuing to rub my back in circles.

Later Lee announced we could take some time out to watch TV. The picture was only black and white, and the motor made it hard to hear, but it was a simple pleasure from home that felt comforting. It was a joy to laugh and feel a connection return to the crew. I had certainly needed it.

The next day around five-pm, we all went on deck to put another reef in the mainsail to slow the boat down, but the wind was too much, so we ended up bringing it down. The rain was bucketing down, so we tied the bottom of the mainsail into a catchment and scooped water out with pots and pans into a bucket and funnelled it into twenty-five litre plastic containers. The water was used for drinking water as we were running dangerously low.

It was pouring down. With my eyes closed, I sat with my tongue out, feeling the sensation of the rain as it landed. I licked my lips, enjoying the flavour of fresh, clean water. I didn't have time to put on wet weather gear, and I was soaked right through to the bone. The cold wind against my skin felt exhilarating. I was drenched, but I felt cleansed of the negativity that had been following me around recently like a thick, black cloud over my head. I smiled the biggest smile.

It was the first time in a long time we were having fun and laughing together. It warmed my heart, watching everyone working hard to collect the water. It was about taking care of each other.

Not only were we grateful to Mother Nature for restocking our water supply, but we were also thankful to have a rain shower after seven days with no wash. Lee had enforced no freshwater showers for the lack of drinkable water on board. The water in the tank from Djibouti tasted dirty and sour, like it had gone putrid. But we had to drink it because Lee didn't buy bottled water.

And even with fresh water, it was impossible to wash on deck because of how dangerous it was to stand because of the rough waves. The rain settled the waves and gave us time to have a quick wash and get ready for whatever Mother Nature had in store for us next.

Chapter 16

Coming face to face with a squall sent shivers down my spine and made me want to shit my pants. The weather had been severe for a few days in a row, to the point it was impossible to hold a pen to paper to write in my journal. On deck, I could see sets of huge fifteen to twenty-metre waves continuously crashing towards the horizon. It looked like we had landed on some strange water planet. I had only seen waves like this in the movies; it was hard to process what I saw in front of me.

Having already covered one thousand five hundred miles, we had one thousand miles to go until we reached Sri Lanka. Smack bang in the middle of the Indian Ocean.

I checked the barometer and watched it drop rapidly, which indicated we were in a low-pressure system. I had heard the weatherman talking about low-pressure systems on TV. Still, I had no idea what they looked like and what it would mean for a sailing boat in the middle of the Indian Ocean. I started asking Brian questions.

"What the fuck is going on?"

"Do you really want to know?"

I thought about it, but I knew I couldn't pretend this time. "Yes, I want to know. I'm petrified, and I can see the barometer has dropped."

He told me straight to my face with fierce directness, "We are on the outskirts of a cyclone, and chances are we will enter it."

My eyes widened and overflowed with tears of fear. Brian told me we didn't have any weather forecasting equipment, which is why we had no information about it.

"Are you fucking serious?!"

Brian pulled me into bed, trying to settle me as the boat thrashed around us.

"Ssshhh! It's going to be okay. We will get through it. The boat is strong and built for this. The crew is capable. This is the time for trust, okay? Do you trust me?" he whispered.

"Yes, I trust you."

"That's good. Lee thinks Nikki and Andy shouldn't know, so they don't freak out. So, keep it to yourself, okay?"

"Okay."

Brian kissed me on the forehead. I think Lee knew Brian had told me just by the glances he gave me. It didn't feel right. Everyone should have the same information. I began to process the fact we were flirting with death. The whole situation was out of my control, so I embraced every moment because I didn't know how much longer I had to enjoy breath in my lungs and the life force in my body.

At one point, I helmed for a couple of hours down ten feet waves, but it became too rough and heavy to surf the boat along them. Brian and Lee needed to do all the helming from then on.

The situation quickly changed from severe to critical. The squalls became frequent, increasing in duration—sudden increases in wind speed that usually involved heavy rain showers and thunderstorms. The squalls banded together on the horizon and approached us like an invasion in the fog. I prayed every time one approached. Think of all those scary movies about "perfect storms." It was exactly like that. Petrifying!

We were heading south, trying to outrun the cyclone, passing through the "safe quadrant," as Brian called it.

It didn't feel very "safe" to me, but if this was the "safe

quadrant," I sure as hell didn't want to see what the "unsafe quadrant" looked like.

The boat was tossed from one side to the other with such force it was impossible to stand in the saloon without having three points of contact at all times. To stay safe, you either had to be lying in bed, rolling around in your lay cloth, sitting on the toilet with all limbs against the walls to avoid pissing all over yourself, or you were sitting in the cockpit tethered to the boat. But wearing safety harnesses was never encouraged or enforced, mainly because we had nothing to attach them to. As the safety lines that acted as a guard rail had been removed for other repairs.

It was soaked inside the saloon because we were constantly going in and out of the hatch in our wet weather gear. I slipped as I was walking in the saloon and slid and fell into the lounge, luckily controlling my body weight. Andy wasn't so lucky. He repeated exactly the same motion but fell against the bench, slamming the side of his chest that left a large purple bruise.

Lee raced on deck to blame me for leaving the hatch open for too long and accused me of causing Andy's injury. Brian held my hand in the dark as Lee stared me down, continuing with his verbal barrage about my negligence. I just sat there, wiping the rain from my face. I held Brian's hand tight and copped it sweet in complete and utter silence.

I knew it wasn't my fault. But I understood my position and knew no one could challenge the skipper. I played along with the game. It was very military. I didn't answer back. I didn't get to be heard. I didn't get to explain. No excuses. The skipper did the talking—or screaming in this case—and the crew shut the fuck up and listened. We did as we were told and got on with it. *Yes, Skipper. No, Skipper. Three bags full, Skipper.*

"Sorry for my negligence Lee."

"Don't apologise to me. Apologise to Andy."

"Okay." I couldn't believe what little came out of my mouth. I apologised to Andy. My strength had transmuted into restraint. If Lee was going to be a rock, I had to be water. I had to flow and flex with his harshness. This was my new secret power. I was in control when I said nothing at all. I had always thought my strength came from speaking up and fighting back, but I was learning something new. I discovered that silence in this context could be just as useful. This was the only way to stop giving my power away to Lee. I knew I needed to save every precious drop of it for when it really mattered.

Lee still cooked dinner, yelling and swearing at Brian to minimise the rocking whilst he cooked with boiling water. It was impossible to keep the boat level in these conditions. Brian and I chuckled at the thought of Lee stressed out being thrown about in the kitchen. Brian wondered why we didn't just eat canned food. I'm sure Brian would've been quite happy living off Spam.

It was sweltering and humid living conditions with all the hatches closed, and it was very smelly and very wet. It smelled like bad breath, wet, damp clothes, and food gone foul. Washing and maintaining standard hygiene levels was impossible because we could not stand in one spot for more than a second. However, the crew made every special effort to brush their teeth twice a day. No one would be game not to after from my experience.

With the wind behind us, we were reaching decent boat speeds. After two days, the sky cleared between squalls. It was a heavy squall line, but the time between them began to increase until we thought we were nearly through it. Respite seemed like it was just around the corner.

Brian and I had been on watch for eight hours whilst Lee worked on repairing the engine. As we were about to change watches, I caught sight of a squall approaching with a band that was thicker and darker than all the others we had encountered over the past week. It began to move stealthily around us. I knew we were in for something very different.

I described to Brian what I saw coming up behind us. Brian immediately turned his head to look. His eyes grew large with concern. The expression he gave me offered no reassurance. This was the one we had been waiting for. I read him loud and clear.

The terror in the air covered me like a wet, heavy blanket that I wanted to hide underneath in the front locker. The darkness approached with such stillness. The sound of a droning hum could be heard in the distance. The waves licked their lips, salivating at the taste of the boat.

It crept up behind us like a stalker before a violent assault. But we knew the enemy was coming. And we were ready to fight. Head on. Face to face. We looked it dead in the eye. My hands felt clammy. Every hair on my body stood up and was ready to run. This was hard-core suspense in real life. A live or die moment. I couldn't help but feel excited by the unexpected. *Come on, motherfucker, I'm ready to dance.*

Brian and I had grown accustomed to the continuous squalls and had even started to enjoy them.

And then the attacker struck. The wind picked up with such ferocity. It slammed Brian in the back of the head, which pushed him forward almost off his feet. Brian had prepared me well in the circumstance that we might come across a dangerous situation such as this one.

"If the wind ever gets too strong and threatens to capsize the boat, you must act quickly with a clear head. You must move safely into position to release the headsail. I will prompt you so you will never have to make that call on your own."

I remembered every word he said. I was ready for this dance. And it was time to turn the music up REAL LOUD.

The grey sky turned to complete pitch-black darkness. I couldn't make out the horizon. I had lost sense of my position in the world. I couldn't make out what was water and what was the sky. The droning of the wind intensified and developed into an ear-splitting witch scream. At one point, I thought my ears had begun to bleed.

The wind was so powerful it held me down against my will. The rain did not settle the waves this time. All I could do was pray nonstop for God to protect the crew, to protect the boat, and to give me the strength to overcome all doubt when it came time to fight. I was as prepared as I was ever going to be for Brian to make the call. One wave was all it would take to send us to a watery grave. We knew that wave was lurking about in the corners of this squall—a voyeur. Just waiting for its chance to kill. And then suddenly, we saw it. It leapt out from the shadows upon us. Its arms outstretched, reaching for our necks.

Brian made the call. I could just make out his words.

"Release the headsail! Release it! Now!"

I was centred, focused, and clear. I pressed through the wind, moving towards the rope. I firmly rooted myself into position on deck in the dark, and with one tough grip and a flick of the wrist, the sail began to release. The rope shot through my hands like a snake made of scorching hot iron. It kept getting caught tangling and twisting, trying to release itself.

We felt the boat rise on to a ninety-degree angle. It reached ready to capsize at any minute. But as the sail released, the attacker's grip began to slip from our throats and the force fell away from the starboard side, easing the boat back down to an even, steady balance.

It felt like each moment was happening in slow motion. The wind claimed the rope and whipped it about the deck. To even try to touch that rope would mean a certain injury. The sail got caught, which meant it couldn't be sheeted in to tighten it up. We had no control over the sail or the power of the wind. Our only choice was to head in the direction the wind was blowing to save the sail and the rig. The sail's flapping was shaking the rigging like it was made of string. Sixteen-millimetre steel rods now looked like spaghetti. The flapping sail was so intense it sounded like a machine gun. My heart stopped, and I don't think I exhaled the entire time as we waited to see whether the whole rig was about to snap in half. All we could do was wait for the squall to pass, to sheet the headsail back in, and to assess the damage. We watched helplessly as the wind thrashed the sail back and forth, slapping it in every direction possible, the wind taking its sweet ass time tormenting us.

Straight after, Brian and I had shouted at each other. But we couldn't understand a word one of us was saying.

I thought I had fucked something up during the release and that the shredded sail was my fault. I had gotten used to being the scapegoat. I could foresee another reason for Lee to direct his aggression my way. *Here we go again*, I thought.

I hadn't noticed because of the action, but Lee had shot up at the moment when I released the headsail and saw the situation for what it was. He could tell from our stressed verbal exchanges that we were extremely escalated and full of adrenaline.

"Hey guys, calm down! It's okay! We'll ride it out!"

Once Lee had sheeted in the headsail, we changed over. I went straight to my room and changed into dry clothes. I waited for Brian to finish talking things over with Lee. My thoughts were racing uncontrollably. *Why did the rope tangle? What did I do wrong? What could I have done differently? Should I have tried to uncoil the rope?*

It would have been impossible. I would have lost a hand. The seriousness of the situation engulfed me. I wanted to cry to release the emotions, but I was numb. I just kept getting visions of looking straight down at the whitewash as the boat tipped on that ninety-degree angle. The ferocious whitewash was like a beast's mouth frothing with anticipation over its next meal. Brian walked into the cabin dripping with water.

"I'm sorry!" I blurted out, exhausted and defeated.

"What for?" he replied.

"I must have fucked something up," I answered.

"You did everything I asked you to. It didn't go smoothly, but the rope was coiled. It wouldn't have gone smoothly for anyone who touched that rope. You remained calm and acted when I told you to. You saved the boat."

I fell silent as I tried to process Brian's words. *It wasn't my fault. I wasn't to blame.*

My heart was still pounding as I laid in bed, and my head hit the pillow. But as the shock began to fade, I couldn't help but think the storm symbolised everything I had run away from. Trust. Pain. Love. Truth. My passion. My power. My forgiveness. But I didn't run away this time. I danced with my demons. Every single shadowy figure that had been trying to mislead me down the dark alleyways of my mind. The storm might have won one round with the sail, but I had defended the boat—my body, mind, spirit, and soul—from the monsters and had triumphed in the face of evil. To survive was not enough. I wanted to dance these motherfuckers into the ground, bury them, and take home the gold.

Brian's words made me realise the rape I experienced could have happened to anyone. I was simply living my life with my sails full of wind until the rape threatened to sink me, and as I tried to release the pressure by running away, the rope coiled. I also realised it didn't matter how many complications happened along the way, as long as I sailed this boat home. I was going to take home that gold. I had nothing to be ashamed of anymore. I could forgive myself because I was never to blame. What happened to me was not my fault.

Just as I was about to fall asleep, I called out to Brian, who was sleeping in the galley. "Brian! If I didn't fuck that up, then you know what that means?"

He laughed. "What does that mean?"

"I FUCKING DANCED!"

"You sure did!"

We both laughed hysterically until we fell asleep exhausted.

Chapter 17

There were three meals left each, which had to last us until we reach Sri Lanka. Brian estimated it could take four days to get there, now that we were clear of the cyclone. Nikki and Andy looked like they were carrying their own broken, heavy spirits on their backs. I could see it in everything they did. Their concentration slipped while keeping course. They gave one-word responses in low tones like the effort to speak was just too much. They moved slowly, hunched over, and heads down. No eye contact. Appearing to have lost interest in anything to do with sailing, preferring to spend their time in their cabins, isolated and alone. I knew the feeling. I gave reassuring smiles hoping to help bring them back into the world of the living.

Without knowing what had occurred in Djibouti, I was still cautious to directly reach out to offer any real support in case it might offend them. There didn't seem to be any privacy on the boat to have a conversation away from Lee. I felt like anything I said could be used against me and invite negative attention. But I was still concerned about my crewmates and cared deeply about their mental health.

I wondered what shit Lee was filling their heads with on their watches. I suspected it might have been his negativity that was feeding their depression.

But I also knew the extreme weather conditions were gruelling and brutal on our bodies. We all felt the impact of the physically demanding schedule and the mental and emotional exhaustion that was required to cope with the uncertainty of possible imminent death. I was sure their heads were filled with the same questions as mine. *Were we going to survive this? Would we ever see land again? Would any of us make it home?* And when you're faced with your own death, anything can happen. You can flight, freeze, or fawn.

The way I saw it, we had three choices on how to cope:

1) We could give up trying, just give in to the situation and our thoughts, and not try to change it;

2) We could leave our bodies, isolate, and try to protect ourselves by withdrawing; or

3) We could fight with everything we had: with our bodies, by sticking together, lifting each other, and most importantly with *optimism*.

We needed *hope* now more than ever. This situation would not get better by chance. We had to change. I had to come back to love, even if it was temporary. I had to try. I had to help. If it was my purpose, what better time to take *action*. I wouldn't be living my truth if I ignored the first situation that came knocking.

I began to worry that Nikki's and Andy's mental health might cause them to veer off course. I was scared about being stuck out in the ocean with no food. We needed to remain focused on getting to the destination. We simply could not afford to waste time. There were no options anymore. We needed each other, and we needed to fight.

The sky was bright blue and mostly cloudless. But we embraced the clouds as they were bringing with them gifts of wind. We had to try anything to gain speed.

One day, we hoisted a spinnaker—one hundred and eighty metres of sail. It was made of super lightweight nylon fabric. When filled with wind, it looked like a huge parachute that ballooned out in front of the boat. The spinnaker pulled the boat along at a slow speed to conserve diesel.

Brian and Lee were the only ones experienced enough to handle the spinnaker. The rest of us worked the ropes on request. I enjoyed the challenge of trying something new. We pulled down the spinnaker in the afternoon, which ended up being a whole lot of trouble. I was told to release the spinnaker and did as instructed but ended up with rope burns on my hand. We couldn't sheet it in fast enough to pull it onto the boat in time, so we had to let it go in the water and then pull it up. Just as we did, the helm broke. It took four hours to fix it, which cancelled out any advantage the spinnaker gave us.

Grrrrrrrr!

Despite this fiasco, everyone appeared to be in much better spirits. Down to the last meal of our food rations, I tried to add whatever I could find in the cupboards to maximise the nutritional content.

The crew were determined to catch fish. We pulled together and worked endlessly on making fishing lures and trying to improve them.

At one point, we thought we had a fish on the line, but instead, we caught a small white plastic bag—*damn plastic pollution.* And it was everywhere in the Indian Ocean! We were constantly dodging floating rubbish.

The ETA kept changing with boat speed and averaged around thirty hours after our last meal. I remained doubtful we could maintain enough speed. Sometimes we only had perfect wind for one or two hours, and then it completely dropped off. I prayed it would keep up. Lee suggested everyone needed to conserve energy.

Brian spoke to me privately. "Conserving energy means no sex for us."

"What? That sucks!" I was disappointed, but I knew the

situation was critical.

Brian hadn't been himself since we came out of the storm. I knew he worried about food intake and its effect on his body, energy levels, and concentration. He confessed he attached the spinnaker upside down.

Lee shouted at him, "What the fuck were you thinking? You fucking idiot!!"

I was helming at the time. It was seriously tense.

"I think I lost concentration because I'm not eating properly," Brian later told me. I believed him.

"I felt so humiliated being spoken to like that in front of you," he said vulnerably.

"I get that. That's how I feel when it happens to me. It's embarrassing."

"I feel helpless that I can't protect you."

"Me too, but hopefully we don't have to put up with him for too much longer," I offered as reassurance.

"Why, are you going to throw him overboard?" Brian attempted to lighten the conversation.

I laughed. "No! I mean, when we arrive in Thailand, we won't have to deal with him anymore."

Brian looked very thin and tired after helming during the storm. He was used to eating three meals a day with double portions. He was devastated after we ran out of our private stash of sweets. Brian pretended he was fine by wearing his smile like a mask. I massaged his muscles daily to help him relax and sleep. I told myself he would be okay.

During our watch, I had a brainwave. There was one onion and a few cloves of garlic left in the cupboard. I could make soup.

"Lee, would it be okay if I made a soup out of the onion, garlic cloves, and spices?"

"Go for it! There's some fajita mix, too; you could throw that in." Lee was pleased with something I said for the first time in a long time.

I made the soup for lunch and used fajita spices, pepper, salt, fish oil, and vegetable oil. It tasted like *hope*. Everyone was pleased to have something in their bellies, and it kept us going.

"The first thing we're doing in Sri Lanka is going to a restaurant for food and beer," Lee announced excitedly.

I couldn't wait. I thought about my friends at home. We used to go out for dinner all the time. I realised how much I took food for granted. What I would have done for anything edible at that point. All I had left to consume was cigarettes, coffee, water, and thoughts about home.

The sound of the kookaburras in the morning. My brother's R&B music thumping on my bedroom wall. Drinking chai tea and eating vegemite on toast outside on my veranda, looking out over the horses in the neighbour's paddock. Watching the eucalyptus trees sway and the leaves rustling with the wind. The heat from the sun on my neck as I play my guitar with the bush landscape as my audience. Lying in front of the wood fireplace late at night, resting my head on my dad's big belly, watching TV as he snores away. Our deep conversations over a couple of beers that I would steal from his bar fridge to replace but never did. And I missed playing with Tilly, our dog. I giggled as memories of home back stroked through my mind.

All-day, the wind teased us as it picked up and dropped off. Brian locked off the helm considering the swell was flat, and sat next to me.

"Just be prepared. It might be four more days until we get there. We don't have enough diesel, and the wind hasn't been consistent."

His words shattered my spirit into a pile of dust. I felt like everything I had worked so hard to keep strong and safe in the harbour of my mind had been smashed on the rocks. I wept as silently as I could. Don't fuck with my hope. *Fuck you, Brian.*

I tried to wipe away my tears before Brian could see the impact of that one sentence. But, of course, he noticed.

"I'm sorry, I'm just a realist."

He tried to reassure me with his usual positive attitude. Still, this time he let his worries and insecurities out for me to see. He had become human. It was okay, and it was beautiful. I didn't need him to be strong anymore. I needed his humanness. He was scared, and that was okay.

"It's alright. Everyone's scared. You're allowed to be too. Come here."

I pulled him in close and held him in my arms with his head on my chest as I stroked his hair.

I looked up at the stars and watched the lights on the planes fly slowly across the sky; I wished I had just flown home like normal people, but I knew I wasn't normal. Whatever was about to happen; I accepted with a gracious heart and a smile on my face because I had given it my everything, and I wasn't going down without a fight.

Chapter 18

It was torture waiting in Galle Marina for the Sri Lankan Navy, who were probably pissing about, trying to scab alcohol and cigarettes off other yachts. It had been forty-eight hours since our last meal. The crew were tired, but we couldn't sleep now that we were so close to food. Finally, the Navy arrived.

Together we collected our shore passes and stepped onto land with no feelings of giddiness. We took tuk-tuks to the bank, did a money exchange, and went straight to a local restaurant.

"Don't eat or drink excessively, guys! Your bodies won't be able to handle it," Lee advised.

His advice was thrown straight out the window. Our appetites were fuelled by the low prices for food and drinks. At dinner, I took my time with my long neck beer, but everyone else went for it hard. I knew I wasn't ready for much alcohol. I could feel my stomach wasn't prepared for it yet. For food, I ordered chicken chop suey and a big dish of vegetables and noodles, and I helped Brian eat his chips. We all had banana fritters and banana pancakes with ice cream and honey for dessert. The food was fantastic! It was paradise after such an ordeal.

The restaurant was right on the beach, so we sat earthing ourselves with our feet in the sand. I felt grateful to be safe on land again. *Thank fucking God.*

Brian, Nikki, and I went for a walk on the beach with our pina coladas in hand. We talked about wanting to be as far away as possible from the boat and Lee. It began to rain, so we stripped off into our underwear and dove into the water to cleanse ourselves of the past few weeks. I swam toward Brian and straddled his back.

"We made it!" I darted a kiss on his cheek.

"Just one leg to go." He kissed my cheek and looked back at the sea.

I gently turned his head towards me.

"But first, let's enjoy where we are now and celebrate how far we've come!"

He laughed, realising he was receiving some reassuring medicine of his own.

"Let's!" he said, lifting me high in the air and throwing me back into the water.

"You Bastard!" I splashed him, laughing as I came up for air with hair in my face.

Brian and I then went for massages, which became more of a creepy rub down than anything. My massage entailed a lot of attention to my buttock region.

With great reluctance, we headed back to the boat for a much-needed warm, refreshing shower. We handed in our laundry to be cleaned, and then Nikki, Andy, Brian, and I went out to a beach bar. I was very pleased to hear Lee wasn't coming. He must have wanted some alone time too.

We continued to eat all night, snacking on omelettes, fried fish, and roti.

"Play any '90s pop music!" Nikki was wasted and demanded the DJ play her favourite cheesy music.

We were playing pool, enjoying cocktails, and sharing enormous spliffs with the locals when Nikki began to break down crying.

"Thank God, we're off that boat! I've not been coping. Not with any of it. The cyclone was terrifying, but Lee's worse!"

She was attracting a lot of attention from the people at the bar. We looked at each other, reluctant to say anything in case it got back to Lee. I tried to take her away from the rest of the crew, but she refused.

"No, I wanna fuckin' talk 'bout this!" she slurred.

I listened as she spoke about how much she hated Lee. However, I avoided verbalising any sentiments against him because I still didn't trust her after Djibouti. I wanted more than anything to connect, to share our experience, and to have a bitch session about Lee, but all I could offer was a silent shoulder to cry on. After all, this was my idea in the first place. I felt responsible for her. She needed to get it all out and off her chest.

"Renee, I have to tell you something. I was the one who got you in shit with Lee. But you don't understand. It's impossible being on watch with him. You have Brian. I have no one, and I need to stay on his good side. I told him some stuff you told me. I didn't know he was going to turn on you like he did. I'm sorry."

"I thought you might have. I get why. You have to survive this trip too. Sometimes you have to become someone you don't like to do that. I get it. I've hurt people before too," I replied, not surprised but pleased she had the courage to tell me the truth.

Nikki's eyes glazed over as she looked up from holding her head in her hands. "And you know what? Lee is a junkie! A fucking junkie! I saw him shoot up on the boat. He uses methadone. A heroin replacement."

I didn't know what to say. I was shocked by her revelation. His behaviour seemed to make sense to me now. It explained his constant mood swings. We all knew Lee smoked weed every day. But this was much more serious. I had no idea how methadone affects someone's brain. My fucking life depended on this guy's expert opinion. If Lee was under the influence of heavy drugs, what control did he have over the situations we encountered? I felt relieved we had Brian. I wondered if Brian knew about this. Surely not.

I could have allowed Nikki to destroy herself that night by letting her tell her story to the whole crew. I could have had my revenge for her stabbing me in the back in Djibouti, but I chose to protect her instead. If Lee found out she had shared his secret with the crew, he would've made life hell for her as he had for me. I did not wish that upon anyone.

"That's really scary, Nikki. We need to get through this together. When we arrive in Phuket, we can finish this conversation, but right now, I think it's best to go back to the boat and have a good sleep. You're fucking exhausted."

Nikki initially resisted my advice as she knew Lee was there, but I told her to be strong, keep her mouth shut, and just go to bed.

In the morning, Brian and I had organised with Lee to have a free day to ourselves. But before we left, I had to check my email for a reply from Steve. It turned out that Steve had so much grace about it. He completely understood that I might meet someone, or I might have a change of heart. He just wanted me to have a great adventure. He knew the power of an epic journey and the awareness adventure could bring if you're open to meet new people and ideas. Steve was light-hearted and placed no expectations on a particular outcome. He understood my heart too. He understood I lived in the moment. He didn't see me meeting someone else as a betrayal. If anything, he saw it as honouring myself and doing what made me happy. It felt amazing to have his support and closure.

I was energised to spend an amazing day with Brian. We needed a break from the crew, and immersing ourselves in the lush, green rainforest and culture was just the right prescription. We had our private air-conditioned mini-van and went exploring a local fruit market. The locals greeted us with kindness and offered samples of different fruits like bananas, oranges, and mangosteens. We stopped for coconuts, sliced open with a machete by the vendor on the side of the dirt road. Brian asked our guide to snap a photo of us on the disposable camera he bought at a local convenience store.

A small old man whose skin told his story of a long, hard-working life tried to sell us souvenirs. I politely declined and smiled at him. I felt guilty. I felt this overwhelming pressure from the local people to give them money.

We stopped to watch water buffalo lazing and grazing on the green grass in the rice fields and visited a tea factory and an Ayurveda spice garden where students learn about herbal medicine. The beaches were gorgeous, with long fishing boats lined up on the shore next to tangled fishing nets, and children jumping off rocks onto the sand.

We finished our day with dinner and drinks at a colourful cocktail bar with pretty hammocks on the beach. They had a wide selection of magazines, so we chilled there, taking time to relax.

The next day the crew went hard on all the cleaning tasks and provisioning. We smashed it. I wanted to surprise the crew and reward them for all their hard work, so I headed out of the marina to pick up curry, samosas, roti, and beers. They appreciated the thought.

Later that night, Lee began to open up about his hardships. "You guys think sailing through that cyclone was hard? I was in Phuket when the tsunami hit in 2004. My friends and I took out our boats looking for survivors, but most of the time, we ended up just picking up dead bodies. Their bodies weren't just dead. They were mangled. Sliced up. Missing limbs. Because of the debris in the water. It was the children that got me."

He described the day in such detail that I pictured it all in my head as if I was there. I felt terrible for him. He had experienced what I could only imagine as being like something out of a war zone. He was clearly traumatised by the experience, and who wouldn't be after seeing such devastation.

"I have nightmares all the time. Their faces haunt me. It doesn't matter whether I'm asleep or awake. They remind me of the ones I couldn't rescue. The dead bodies I had to let go of to make space for survivors. I have to do whatever I can to go on living. It has been the hardest years of my life."

Strangely, I envied his experience not for his suffering or because I wanted to see what he had seen but because I wanted to help people like he had done one day. Lee was a *hero*. He had made a real, meaningful contribution with his life, but at what cost? In comparison, I hadn't made a meaningful contribution to life as yet. But Lee also didn't know the experiences that I had survived in my life. And it was unfair to compare storms.

Lee had experienced the impact of a tsunami. He not only survived, but he also put his fears aside to get involved and save the lives of many he could have left to die. He deserved *respect*. It made me realise the old sage was true, "You never know what battle a person is facing." And that's why it's important to be kind to everyone. Lee was mean because he was in a lot of pain. It didn't give him an excuse to be an "asshole," but I certainly understood why he wasn't having a good time inside of that mind of his, and I could relate to that.

"Can I give you a hug? You've had a tough run, but you're a hero. I hope you know that."

Lee smiled somewhat bashfully and accepted my hug.

The next morning, Lee came into my cabin.

"Pack your things. You and Brian are going to Hikadua for the night."

What? Lee had given us permission to leave the boat and spend the night there. The surprise came out of nowhere! *Is he starting to like me? Is this a reward for Brian? Is this appreciation for staying strong during the storm? Or is it for working hard on the boat the past few days whilst the others nursed hangovers?* It didn't matter why. I was quietly jumping around inside at the idea of spending a night off the boat. I packed as quickly as possible, but I couldn't help feeling guilty for Andy and Nikki as they weren't receiving any special privileges.

We organised the tuk-tuk to pick us up in the morning at nine-thirty.

It was pouring down rain, but it was the first time in a long time I felt free. Free from the boat. Free from the crew, but more importantly, free from the command of Lee. I held my hand open, catching the rain. I tilted my head back and breathed in the smell of Sri Lanka. The rain was washing me clean and reviving my spirit. Brian held my hand tight and pulled me in close to him, excitedly kissing me on the forehead with joy. We were so happy to finally be alone together.

We arrived at a sleepy guesthouse on the beach that Lee had recommended and asked for a room overlooking the beach. It had a queen-size bed with mosquito netting draped from the ceiling. Anywhere was romantic after sleeping on a sailing boat for two months. It was simple. It had a cabinet, side table, and a small bathroom. No TV and no air conditioning. It was simply perfect.

We sat on the balcony appreciating nature's bounties: the sounds of the rain on the roof, the natural patterns the droplets made in the sand, the way the palm trees swayed with the wind, and the peaceful calm of not having to be anywhere or to be anything but ourselves.

Brian went inside to pour a drink. I followed him and closed the door gently behind me, sliding the lock. I slowly took my dress off. My naked silhouette stood self-assured in front of the bed. A silver light between the curtains found its way onto my spine as I laid on the bed. I looked up at Brian, glowing. Our eyes connected. Brian looked as though he was admiring every crevice of my skin. I breathed a long exhale. He stirred towards me and knelt in front of the bed to kiss my lips. He kissed me softly on the neck, running his fingertips down my back and guiding me into his embrace as he lifted me around his waist. The white sheets wrapped around us and fell to the floor as we made love.

There was a blackout as dark descended, so we lit candles and put them in long neck bottles while we finished a bottle of arak.

The next morning, we scraped together the very little money we had to pay for our accommodation, breakfast, tuk-tuk driver, and a pair of shorts because my last pair were about to fall apart. We had no money to pay for our laundry. Our guide fancied one of Brian's shirts and took it without asking, so Brian bargained with him.

"Waive the cost of our laundry, and you can keep the shirt."

He accepted.

We waited until two-pm for the Navy to board the boat and sign us out of Sri Lanka. Still trying to scab cigarettes after they took four packets from my wardrobe when we checked in. I was furious. Fucking thieves. But what could I do? After a lot of waiting, we were finally given the all-clear.

We headed back into the unpredictable hands of the Indian Ocean. I was filled with the familiar feeling of uneasiness about the unexpected. *What did the ocean have in store for us this time?*

Hopefully, not a great deal. The crew was nervous about running into bad weather again. And no amount of time in Sri Lanka could have given us the rest we needed and deserved.

I whispered prayers into the breeze as we sailed out. I just wanted to go home now. We all did. *Mother Nature, please help us home.*

Step 6. Run Wild, You're Free, Laugh Loudly

"Your task is not to seek for love, but merely to see and find all the barriers within yourself that you have built against it."

RUMI

Chapter 19

Welcome to the world of the doldrums. Water that looked like an enormous glass mirror covered in expensive diamonds that sparkled in the sun's reflection. It was one of the most spectacular landscapes I had ever seen—the only downside, not a whisper of wind. We had been motoring for the past thirty-six hours. We had a strong current pushing against us and a lot of traffic from the shipping lanes and fishing boats pestering us.

Brian and I had been talking about Lee's offer to work with him as second-in-command in Phuket when a swarm of enormous dragonflies swept over the boat and buzzed around all the lights. We turned the lights off downstairs. Brian volunteered to take the sail down. I had never seen him wriggle and squirm so much, just like I had when I thought there was a cockroach in my underwear. I chuckled at him having the heebie-jeebies as I pulled the string on my hoodie tightly closed around my face. I did not want any of those things going down my jumper. Brian waved his hands around in an attempt to "shoo" them away and smacked at the sail to get rid of them.

"I can feel them all over me. They're even flying up my shorts!" he cried out.

"You love it!" I laughed, amused by Brian's performance.

Once the sail was pulled down, it looked like it was alive as it moved and rattled with the mass of dragonflies caught inside it.

"We could rent a place in Phuket together! It could be fun," he exclaimed.

"I don't want you to get your hopes up. Just in case Lee

doesn't come through. Remember how Lee sold us this trip. Just take everything he says with a grain of salt."

I tried to keep my voice down in case anyone was listening. I wanted everything to work out for Brian. I planned to spend some time with him in Phuket, whatever the outcome. But with each passing day, I longed to be in the company of my family and friends. I cared so much for Brian, but I felt conflicted. I couldn't just abandon him in Phuket. I also couldn't tell him I wanted to go straight home after the trip was over. I felt like the water was circling in around me, and I wanted to run home.

Andy spoke about running low on money. He planned to stay with Lee.

"I don't even have a place for myself, Andy! I moved out when I left for Gibraltar. We will probably just have to stay on the boat until I find another place."

That sounded shit. I was sure the boat would be the last place he would want to stay.

Lee continued, "I'm going straight back to work. I'm looking forward to showing Andy around Phuket and catching up without having the pressures of the delivery."

"I have absolutely no cash, so my dad is buying me a plane ticket to Chiang Mai, where he lives with his Thai wife and family. I'm not sure what that's going to be like. But I'm looking forward to spending time with my dad," added Nikki.

"I can get my old waitressing job back at home, and Dad bought me a car. I'm looking forward to hanging out with my family and friends. I'll head back home after Brian sets himself up in Phuket," I shared.

Brian looked pleased.

In the morning, big black clouds hovered above us. It brought back bad memories of the storm. Fear grabbed me by the throat at the thought of enduring those conditions again, which gave me a splitting headache and made me want to throw up.

"There's hardly any chance of that happening again, considering where we're positioned in the Indian Ocean." Brian gave me a detailed meteorology explanation of why. He could have said anything, and I would have believed him. I had no idea what he was saying. I told him that too. It helped, though. Shortly after, the wind came around too much. We ended up on a course of one hundred and thirty degrees when Phuket was on a course of eighty degrees. We decided to motor sail to avoid wasting time on a wrong course too far south that would push us towards Sumatra, which is renowned for its squall conditions and strong southerly currents this time of year. *Fuck that right off.*

I showed cracks now and again, as soon as any uncertainty arose. Out of nowhere, I would have verbal outbursts. "I'm sick of this fucking shit!"

Brian laughed at my moodiness but understood the feeling and always attempted to lighten me up. We were a great team. Always able to lift each other. I had figured out there were three things that could depress Brian: when there wasn't enough food, he needed a sugar fix, or a dish was served with only two ingredients.

~

One day, Lee befriended a baby falcon that landed on the boat. The falcon let Lee pick it up, and it found a spot to rest on his hand with its claws digging into him. Falcons were supposed to be dangerous to humans. Lee named it "Jiffy." The crew spoke about nothing else but the bird. It was gorgeous, its feathers the colour of desert sand and brown bark.

I couldn't help but wonder if there was more to this bird than its beauty. Lee allowed it to sleep in the saloon, which made me feel uneasy. The falcon started off eating cockroaches. There were plenty of them, so there was no chance he would go hungry.

It opened one eye at any slight movement and stared at me as I brushed my teeth. It reminded me of Lee keeping watch of the crews' every move. Lee would just sit at his control desk, staring at it. It was weird. Lee spent all his time with the falcon, sitting on the deck, stroking its feathers and talking to it. I told him he looked like a pirate with his pet falcon. He had been talking of keeping it as a pet in Phuket. *Good luck with that.*

I stayed away from the bird. Everyone else touched it, but I was not prepared to put my health at risk. Not again. I didn't want bird flu. No thanks. However, it was nice to see the gentler side of Lee.

Provisions were tight again on this leg. Lee allowed us one meal a day, usually with only two ingredients. Poor Brian. Pasta and one can of tuna to share between the five of us. I was thin. The crew looked gaunt. I could feel my sitting bones pressing painfully against the surface of the seat in the cockpit.

We no longer fit into any clothes we started the trip with. Our pants no longer stayed up on our hips, and we tied a string around our waists as a makeshift belt. Our singlets and shirts began to swim on us. It was a joke. Surely, the owner who was paying the expenses would treat the crew with more respect than this. After all, we were delivering his precious boat. *Is Lee spending all the expense money, or is he keeping some for himself and skimming on provisions? Is he not asking the owner for enough, leaving us short and putting our lives at risk?* There was no excuse for this anymore; it was irresponsible conduct on the skipper's behalf.

Much to the crew's disappointment, we were again down to our last rations: a few packets of noodles. Lee fed the bird a packet. It licked at it, and that was it, but enough for it to be wasted. Lee was more concerned about saving the bird than feeding his crew. We had no food for forty-eight hours.

Lee began working on a DVD to give us as a souvenir of the trip. It was terrific but very fake. He made the trip look effortless. He captured the crew always smiling and laughing. Sightings of dolphins. The fish we caught. The beautiful sunsets. *It's the highlight reel, and it's bullshit.*

It was a nice piece of creative work that would go perfectly with the rest of his propaganda. He finished it and gave us all a copy. We were hungry for food and not interested in giving Lee accolades for his creative piece of work.

~

The falcon died early one morning. Lee was devastated. It was like he had just lost his best friend in a sudden accident. I could see the hurt in his eyes. It seemed death was something that shook him to the bone. I wondered if he blamed himself as he did for the lives he couldn't save in the Tsunami. I pretended to care about the death of the bird, but I didn't; instead, I cared about making it home alive myself. The death of the falcon was inevitable. Falcons don't just land on boats and let humans treat them as household pets. But I did care for Lee's anguish. I could see how it had twisted him up inside.

Determined to get us to Phuket as fast as I could, I took ownership of the helm all day. No one was touching it. No one was veering off course. We were not losing a second of time.

I caught sight of land and was over the moon with happiness but kept it to myself as I didn't want to seem disrespectful over the sombre mood that had been cast upon the boat by Lee's grief. I wanted to celebrate with the crew and crack open champagne (metaphorically speaking) to mark the end of the journey. This was the day we had all been waiting for, and we couldn't even enjoy these final hours.

I had land in sight for a good hour until I felt comfortable to quietly tell the crew. I could see the look in everyone's eyes. They shared the same feelings as I had. Lee was still holding onto the dead bird, stroking it. We wanted to scream and jump around, and as we turned to face Lee he was holding the bird's wing out to cut a feather for himself. He took the bird to the side of the boat and lowered himself as close to the water as possible, and let it float away behind us. He watched it until it was no longer in sight.

The crew pumped up the dinghy as the most amazing fluorescent pink filled the sky in pure prettiness, and the mountains of Phuket became clearer. It was a perfect end to the journey, better than any "Welcome Home!" banner. This was Mother Nature's gift for overcoming her tests.

I was obsessed with this time of day. I don't think I missed a sunset on the deck, even if it wasn't my watch. I had to collect every single one and store it away somewhere in my memories to recall when I needed a happy place to go. The sun was my clock. The sun was time. A reminder of how far I had come and how far I still needed to go. It gave me a place to measure where I stood amid the chaos of life. I could just stop, be still, and reflect. Be present. To acknowledge what was going on for me. To check-in with myself and course-correct if need be.

I remember knowing every sunset was another sunset closer to home. I would sing "Comin' Home" by City and Colour. This song spoke to me. It's about travelling all over the world but preferring to be at home, waking up beside a special someone, breathing in their familiar scent, but tormented that the special someone had left them. The song talks about the need to take risks in life but questions the point of taking risks if it means sacrificing love.

Maybe that's what I was slowly discovering. The risks are very much necessary. The adventure, exploring our world, but the external wasn't as important as the internal. Taking in all those extraordinary places and landscapes. Taking stock of the strengths we gain from every experience. Following our dreams, but at the end of the day, coming home to that special someone. That special someone was *my power.*

I needed to cultivate this love inside of me to not only keep my boat afloat but to put wind in my sails. Without that love, my ship was falling apart! I was losing parts and breaking down along the way. But I also needed to shed parts to transform from who I was into someone *better.* Someone *braver.* Someone *stronger.* Someone *wilder.* Someone *freer.* Who laughed LOUDER!

And as I sailed that boat into Nai Harn Beach in Phuket, I knew I had won. I savoured the joy of not only an amazing physical victory but an emotional one too. Just like the name of our boat suggested those WHO DARE WIN.

Chapter 20

Fuck immigration!

We were starving. We lowered ourselves into the dinghy and set off for land. A wave turned the dinghy over, drenching the crew. No one cared. We deserved a beer.

No banks were open, and no one had cash, so Lee took us to a place where we could run a tab. I couldn't believe after everything Lee had put us through, he didn't offer to pay for a celebration dinner to mark the end of the trip. It was the least he could do. My dislike for him was growing by the day, and now it seemed by the hour—minute by minute. Second, by second. Breath by breath. I still wasn't free until I had my bag on my back and off the boat.

We went to a cool reggae bar with many instruments to jam with and then drank as much beer as we could. I picked up a guitar and went off by myself. It was nice to finally be alone.

We returned to the boat around midnight. I slept like a baby.

The next morning, Brian and I put our passports and key cards in a dry bag and jumped off the boat into the refreshing crystal-clear green water and swam to shore. It reminded me of a scene out of the movie *The Beach* with Leonardo DiCaprio, where his character and a French couple swim to a secret island searching for a tropical paradise.

We ran into Andy, who was still drunk from the night before. We joined him for breakfast and then spent the day exploring Phuket on motorbikes, stopping at any bar that looked interesting. We played with naughty gibbons who tried to steal people's sunglasses and pretended to ride parked motorbikes.

In the afternoon, we returned to Nai Harn beach to find the boat was gone. *What the fuck.*

The night before, I had overheard Lee mention he wanted to move the boat, but he never said when or where. I realised I didn't give a shit about my things. I had my passport and money. That's all I needed to get a flight home. I was happy to leave with the clothes on my back if I had to. We decided not to worry about it until the next day.

Andy was still in the same place we left him in the morning, so we invited him to join us in hitting Patong for a night out. We ran out of money during the peak of our night. Conveniently, we ran into a Thai woman who had taken a liking to Andy earlier in the evening. She invited us to drink at her friend's bar and pay the next day.

I was in my element, dancing in the bar with the local ladies. Phuket was famous for prostitution, and this bar was definitely, as the tourists called it, a "girly bar."

Brian suggested we sleep on the beach, but the bar owner offered us a place to sleep. We thought that was very kind but knew she just wanted to keep an eye on us until we paid our bill.

The next day, with enormous hangovers, we paid our bill and set off in search of our boat. Andy recalled the name of a bar Lee liked to hang out at. We followed his lead. The bar owner was expecting us. He told us Lee had been in the night before drinking, telling tales about our adventure. The constant mechanical failures, the cyclone, and food shortages.

Nikki was still passed out on the couch. I went over to check her pulse. She was alive.

The bar owner shouted us a beer. He called Lee and told him we were waiting for him. We couldn't believe we found him. Lee showed up an hour later, off his face on drugs. Nikki told us he had been shooting up methadone since they arrived.

Everyone in that bar looked suspicious to me. They looked me up all over and praised Brian for "picking a beauty." Like I wasn't even human. They reduced me to a mere object Brian possessed. *Fuck off, creeps.*

The whole place gave me the heebie-jeebies. I overheard a few of their stories that frightened me. If this was the company Lee kept, then I wanted off the boat more than ever. This bar was where the devil drank.

That night I wanted to pack my shit up and leave, but Brian convinced me to relax. To officially get our passports stamped to enter the country, we needed to spend the night on the boat, and then we could move off first thing in the morning. It was probably the most challenging part of the trip, but it was everything I had been practising. *Staying* when things are hard and not running away.

Breathe. I could manage one more night.

At sunlight, I woke Brian. We packed our things to leave, and for the last time, we waited for Lee to wake up to visit immigration to legally sign the crew into the country. We knew Lee would sleep forever, considering the state he was in the night before. Brian and Andy sat, contemplating waking him up. Brian asked what I thought would be the best strategy.

"Just go in there and wake him up!" I snapped in some guttural exorcist voice.

This lit a fire under Brian's feet, dashing straight into Lee's cabin to tell him the crew were ready for immigration. I was not in the mood to fuck around. We waited on deck for Lee to emerge from below.

Everyone was quiet as Lee drove the dinghy into port. Immigration processed our passports at a snail's pace, but finally, we were stamped into the country. I kissed my passport. Lee and Andy went to a local bar. No chance. I was getting off the boat *now*, with or without Brian. I told Lee I was moving off the boat. Brian and Nikki followed. Lee suggested we meet for drinks later that night. Brian politely agreed. I wasn't interested but kept that to myself. Lee told us if we were going to use the dinghy, we needed to buy more fuel for it. We didn't. We threw our bags into the dinghy as fast as we could.

Nikki was fucking around. I was ready to explode. I was seething with resentment towards her and allowing myself to fully feel her betrayal during the trip.

"Nikki, I hate how we didn't take care of each other. I hated that we lost each other over Lee's bullshit. We allowed that to happen. We could have done better. We could have been braver. To speak up together. We didn't have each other's back. Maybe it felt like I abandoned you when I got with Brian, but you threw me under the bus with Lee. And that's fucked. I don't hate you. But I don't want to be friends anymore either."

"Renee, I did it to survive him. You have no idea what it was like on watches with him."

"Nikki, please get your shit on the dinghy as fast as you can because I need to get off this boat now and as far away from Lee as possible."

Nikki threw her bag onto the dinghy and jumped in after it. "Me too. I'm sorry, Renee."

"I'm sorry too."

As Brian drove away on the dinghy, I looked back at the boat and finally realised I was free. It was over. I was amazed at how a fifty-three-foot ship could transport us through such a massive experience. It was done. I had finished what I'd started.

I could already see my friends celebrating with their glasses held high, congratulating me on such a huge achievement. I didn't feel proud. But I felt exhausted. I didn't feel like a hero. I didn't feel like I had just completed something amazing. I felt fragile. I felt vulnerable, and I felt raw. I felt like a shipwreck inside. I realised it was okay to feel this way. I had just gone through a massive journey. It was understandable I wasn't bouncing off the walls. I needed time to see things clearly again. Survivors don't regain their power straight away. It comes in waves. Healing is *feeling*, and it takes time. And time heals.

Brian and I walked slowly and quietly up the main street, holding everything we owned on our backs and in desperate need of a shower.

I called my mum at an internet cafe. When I heard her voice, I broke down crying. Falling to my knees, I sobbed. A tidal wave of emotion engulfed me, and at one point, I thought I was drowning in my tears. The entire internet cafe stared at me and listened in as I told Mum about the challenges of the sailing trip. I didn't care. I just wanted to be home. She told me I was *safe*.

Brian and I had a magical month renting a place in a small village. We made love every morning and ate double portions of street food at night. Brian's only request was that all meals had more than two ingredients. It didn't take long for our bodies to return to feeling healthy again. I recuperated whilst Brian was at work, hooning around Phuket on a motorbike in my bikini with the wind in my hair. Free to explore and relax on the quieter beaches with my journal. The smell of the earth was my new addiction.

But I was never going to fully reclaim the power that was rightfully mine until I dislodged the bone that had been stuck in my throat. I needed to talk about what had happened to me. Not what happened on the boat. I needed to speak about the rape. I needed to tell someone. *I was ready.*

Chapter 21

I felt torn about leaving Brian in Phuket. It felt easy being with him. But I had this painful longing to return home. I told Brian it was time that I booked the flight. The flight was in two days. Suddenly, the fairy tale romance was coming to an end. It felt real. I hated this part.

Brian was strong and took the news well. He understood I had to go home, even though he didn't know the full extent behind it. He respected that I needed to go home for my peace of mind as much as it hurt. Brian organised a taxi to the airport and came to see me off. Holding my hand tightly as he had done in Sardinia, he urged me not to cry and reassured me we would be together somehow.

We discussed options like returning to live in Phuket when I felt ready or Brian moving to Australia. We wanted to make it work, but we also accepted that it might not. We both understood the rhythm of life.

We left each other with the mutual understanding we were not together from now on. We appreciated each other as romantics, and we didn't want to make promises we couldn't keep. It was as good as break-ups could be.

He walked me to the departure gate, pulled me close towards him with such passion, and kissed me deeply. We inhaled each other for what felt like the last time. His hands were lost in my hair. I didn't know how I was going to find the strength to walk away. But I did.

Brian pulled me close one last time and whispered in my ear,

"Don't look back. You did it. You're going home."

I cried for the entire eight-hour plane trip home. The other passengers must have thought someone had died. But I guess someone had died. I had died, and I was going home a better person for it. I gave myself the gift of time to get curious about my pain. To explore it. To discover new insights. Yes, I ran away. It was the right decision for me. It gave me time to reflect. Time to myself. Time to break open. Time to lick my wounds. Time to transform. Time to heal. And the healing would continue. It was a lifelong process, one I was now committed to giving space, stillness, love, and time to.

I thought by changing places, countries, and relationships, I could avoid the pain, but getting close to it was the only way to live with it. I had to make love to it. Some people make pilgrimages, go on silent meditations, seek peace in nature, sing chants, do yoga, live in a cave for three years, three months, and three days. I wasn't mature enough to understand any of that when I was twenty-one. Still, I believe this was the way the universe called me to heal in a language I understood.

It was the first time I had ever really crawled out of my pond. This allowed me to gather the bones I had been carrying for so long. It brought all my monsters to the surface. And I learned to dance with them. And I would keep on dancing with them to discover the sea that lived within me.

I was a skipper in control of what course I was on and where I was heading. If I wanted to go fast, I could go it alone, but if I wanted to go far, I needed a solid crew. I didn't want to go fast anymore. I didn't want to do it on my own, either. I needed to choose a solid crew to help keep the ship afloat in times of severe weather warnings. My confidence put wind in my sails to take me wherever I wanted. I didn't want to run away anymore. I wanted to run toward. Toward everything that scared me.

As the plane flew over the Blue Mountains, I began to smile, realising I had one more thing left to do.

I ran as fast I could through the Sydney arrival gates into the open, loving arms of Mum and Dad.

The first thing that came out of my mouth. "Hey guys, when we get home, I have to tell you something that happened to me. And you don't have to do anything. I just need you to listen and believe me, please."

Acknowledgements

To my friends and family, I couldn't have pulled this off without you. The trillion times I picked up this project over the past ten years and told you I was working on my book again, you never stopped believing that I could and would finish it. You are one hell of a fiercely protective cheer squad, full of strong, wise women and men that inspire me to be a better person than I was the day before. Thank you for not giving up on me, offering your kind words of encouragement, and answering my late-night calls. I have appreciated every moment of your time, belief, and unwavering support. You know who you are, and I love you so much!

Mum, thanks for inspiring my creativity from a young age. It's taken on many forms from drama, to poetry, to music, to visual art, and to writing. As a little girl, I used to watch you experiment with your artistic interests. It was like magic how you could create something so pretty out of nothing. It put a big smile on your face, and it made me want to experience that same feeling. It gave me permission to play and express myself. Art has saved my life many times. Thank you for teaching me such an important skill. I love you.

Dad, when something happens that affects me, it's you I want to call and share it with. Even if you're asleep and even if it's 3 am. I know I'm a pain in the ass, but this pain in the ass loves you for always answering the phone and your bias perspective that I can never do wrong. I love you.

Sascha, you've put up with my energy highs and my depressive lows. Thank you for always listening to me when I've needed to share. Even when you've been exhausted, you've always given me time, patience, and love, and during the hardest times, you're the person who shows up. Thank you for reminding me

I'm loved, worthy, and needed in this world. I will always fight for you. I love you.

Jacqui, you taught me true, loving, loyal friendship. You believed me without question when I told you about the sexual assault. I always have a safe place to talk with you. And your words have some kick to them. Thank you for always protecting me, even when it felt like my entire world was under attack. Keep shining. I love you.

Mitch, our relationship is a beautiful piece of art that has transformed us in many ways and shown us parts of ourselves we might not have otherwise known. There is magic between us, whether we like it or not. We always find our way back to each other because there's always something our relationship can teach us. Thank you for adoring me at my best, shining a torch in my darkness, for giving me the space, time, and patience that I've needed to grow, and for accepting even the parts you don't understand because it has helped me to love them more. I love you.

Tim, I appreciated and enjoyed your excitement over my book. I have loved throwing around ideas with you. I know your year hasn't been easy, and your heavy heart has given me a sense of urgency to get this message out into the world. I know sharing this process with you has brought us closer. It fills my heart up, to hear that my work inspires you. Then, as your big sister, I must be doing something right. I love you.

Jake, I miss you every day. Everything I do, I do it for you. I know you're watching over me. Your love reminds me I'm never alone. It's your memory that inspires me to never take a moment for granted, to treasure the ones I love, and to put my life to good use. Thank you for the most painful lessons. I love you.

Nan, thanks for always asking me, "When are you going to

finish that book?" I couldn't let you down. I'm not sure it's what you had in mind, but I'm grateful for your push. I love you.

Mina, my furry friend, and pet soul mate, you have not left my side the *entire* time I have worked on this book! Now that's support. You witnessed every fucking emotion necessary to tell this story. Thank you for your loyalty, looks of concern, and not going to bed until I do. Sometimes I wonder who did the rescuing. I love you.

Danielle, my book coach, you called me out on the story I was not telling. You made me feel safe and supported as I bled over the pages to tell the story I desperately wanted to liberate from my bones. You believed in me to get to the heart of my message. With your guidance, I could dive into the depths of my soul to find it and safely return "home." I love you.

Last, thanks to the people that smile at strangers. Keep smiling at strangers. I know what your smile means to someone struggling. And smiles can save lives. Thank you. I love you.

About the Author

 **Renee Marie Simpson** is a Counsellor, Youth & Community Development Thought-Leader, Speaker, Group Facilitator, and Advocate for deep-level change in societal attitudes and behaviour to support safer communities for women and children. Renee develops partnerships between the government, education providers, and support services. To create support programs that encourage help-seeking and build resilience in people that need it most.

Renee's work is driven by her powerful desire to live and work in ways that leave a legacy of healing and liberation for generations to come.

Renee replenishes exploring healing modalities, philosophies, and perspectives. She enjoys her many creative outlets such as art and poetry, adventures in nature with friends and family, travel, reading non-fiction, and spending quality time with her furry friend, Mina.

Renee is loving pregnancy and looks forward to the birth of her daughter in June.

Renee would love to hear from you and connect.
https://reneemariesimpson.com
@reneemariesimpsonauthor

Printed in Great Britain
by Amazon

21126392R00103